BIG GAME SHOOTING RECORDS

TOGETHER WITH BIOGRAPHICAL NOTES AND
ANECDOTES ON THE MOST PROMINENT BIG GAME
HUNTERS OF ANCIENT AND MODERN TIMES

BY

EDGAR N. BARCLAY

*ILLUSTRATED FROM
PHOTOGRAPHS*

H. F. & G. WITHERBY
326 HIGH HOLBORN, LONDON, W.C.

PREFACE

THE compilation of a book of this nature is only made possible by the assistance of many individuals in supplying information and by consulting the works of others.

My most grateful thanks are therefore due to the correspondents in this and other countries who have furnished me with statistics, and I also tender my acknowledgments to the authors and publishers of the books I have consulted, a list of which is given at the end of the book. The columns of " The Field ", " Country Life ", and other publications have also yielded a great deal of information. Lastly, but by no means least, I have to thank Messrs. Rowland Ward Ltd. for much valuable assistance.

Throughout the book I have purposely refrained from using the prefix " the late " in connection with those sportsmen who are no longer with us, and I have not attempted to bring up to date the titles and rank of the many individuals mentioned, the dates of the bags or episodes with which they are concerned being sufficient by which to identify them.

E. N. B.

CONTENTS

		Page
PREFACE		5
INTRODUCTORY		11

Chap
I. AFRICAN ELEPHANTS		17
II. ASIATIC ELEPHANTS		46
III. AFRICAN BUFFALOES . . .		61
IV. ASIATIC BUFFALOES . . .		67
V. AFRICAN RHINOCEROSES . . .		76
VI. LIONS		92
VII. TIGERS		106
VIII. OTHER AFRICAN GAME ANIMALS .		125
IX. OTHER INDIAN GAME ANIMALS .		137
X. WILD BOAR		152
XI. RED DEER		161
XII. ROE-DEER		186
XIII. CHAMOIS		193
XIV. EUROPEAN BISON . . .		202
XV. ELK		212
XVI. OTHER EUROPEAN GAME ANIMALS .		219
XVII. AMERICAN BISON		228
XVIII. MOOSE		236
XIX. WAPITI		240
XX. NORTH AMERICAN BEARS . .		245
XXI. OTHER NORTH AMERICAN GAME ANIMALS		252
XXII. SOME RECORDS OF ALL SORTS .		264

LIST OF PLATES

GROUP OF LIONESSES APPROACHING IN SINGLE FILE . . . *Frontispiece*

W. D. M. BELL . . . *To face page* 22

HERD OF ELEPHANTS IN THE NILE SWAMPS OF THE SOUTH SUDAN . . „ 44

SIR SAMUEL W. BAKER . „ 56

WILLIAM COTTON OSWELL . „ 82

H.I.M. THE KING-EMPEROR SHOOTING IN NEPAL IN 1911 . . . . „ 108

F. C. SELOUS . . . „ 126

SHOOTING DEER AT A DRIVE WITH LONG BOWS AND CROSS BOWS ABOUT 1400 „ 162

EUROPEAN BISON AT JANKO- WITZ, UPPER SILESIA . „ 202

G. J. VAN HEEK, JR. . . „ 218

BULL MOOSE . . . „ 236

WAPITI BULL, NEAR BANFF „ 244

INTRODUCTORY

THE production of a book bearing the title " Big Game Shooting Records " may not seem quite in keeping with modern ideals, and some may be inclined to regard it as inimical to the best interests of sport. I have, however, so often seen and heard the names of various men mentioned in connection with one and the same record, that I determined, if only for the sake of historical accuracy, to endeavour to obtain the true facts regarding the record bags of the principal animals of the chase. Whatever our views on the subject may be, it seems certain, that so long as the man exists who inherits the natural instinct to hunt, so long will he be interested in the results achieved by others. Records for the mere sake of records are certainly to be condemned, but in every form of blood sport we still regard the blank day as the unsuccessful day, and the day on which we fill the bag as the successful one, and so long as we retain this point of view, game books and hunting diaries will continue to be of interest. A number of the achievements here recorded can never again be equalled, and as examples of skill, courage and endurance, many of them are sufficiently remarkable to merit being placed on permanent record for these reasons alone.

BIG GAME SHOOTING RECORDS

As books of reference dealing with records, we already have Rowland Ward's " Records of Big Game", the one and only authoritative work dealing with horn, antler and other measurements, and Mr. H. S. Gladstone's " Record Bags and Shooting Records " which deals exclusively with small game, but, so far as I know, no attempt has hitherto been made to collect and place on record the most noteworthy bags of big game.

In the compilation of this volume one difficulty was to decide what animals to include and what to leave out. It would obviously be of no interest to anyone to give details of the slaughter of say zebras, giraffes, or any of the small gazelles, nor would such animals as the markhor or ovis poli prove any more interesting, since in these cases good heads are the hunter's sole ambition and numbers mean simply nothing at all. The most obviously interesting records are those concerning dangerous game. Among animals of this type it will be noted that I have not devoted a chapter to leopards or any of the smaller cats. They figure in various bags that are recorded, but they are rarely made the special objective of any hunting expedition and the shooting of them is usually incidental to the hunting of some other animal.

With regard to non-dangerous game, some surprise may be evinced at the inclusion of a chapter devoted to roe-deer, but though this beautiful little animal is usually treated with scant respect in our own islands, it affords first-rate sport to more Continental sportsmen than any other game animal and is nearly as highly prized as the red deer. I trust therefore that the records of Continental bags obtained by stalking or " still hunting" will prove of interest. The European bison still maintains a precarious footing in Europe, though its range and numbers are I believe more strictly limited than ever. The few pages I have devoted to it may be of some historical interest.

The wholesale slaughter of the North American bison cannot by any stretch of the imagination be looked upon as sport. It was purely a commercial proposition for those engaging in it, but it is a scrap of the world's history, the like of which can never be repeated, so I have included a few facts and figures relating to that mighty wave of destruction.

Writing as an historian, I neither praise nor condemn the feats and figures I have collected together; but in reading the pages that follow one should not lose sight of the fact that many of the great bags recorded were made in countries that were then new and practically unknown. The feelings and views of the early pioneers, first penetrating lands where practically every factor was an unknown quantity, cannot be easily visualized to-day. It is hardly surprising however that men endeavouring to carve a career for themselves under such circumstances should have taken a heavy toll of the game. There is no doubt whatever that in Africa the feeding of the natives on game killed by white men has again and again played an all important part in early exploration and colonization. In the middle of the last century, that great hunter and explorer, William Cotton Oswell, on arriving in the country of the Ba-Kaa found them in a pitiable condition. Their crops had failed and they were starving. The chief begged him to feed his people and he took six hundred men, women and children, with him to the hunting grounds. They started in an awful state of emaciation and sickness but in seven weeks he sent them back to their kraals, plump and happy, with not one ill or missing. Can it be wondered that the savage welcomed the white man, and it is certainly difficult to say how much we owe to the influence of the pioneer hunters in the subsequent colonization of the countries in which they first hunted. Those days have gone, never to return, and the unrestricted use of the rifle is practically a thing of the past. As trustees of the world's fauna, civilized man

INTRODUCTORY

has tackled this difficult task with a large measure
of success, and though, unhappily, the realization
of his responsibilities came too late to save
from extermination a few interesting species, the
preservation of wild life is now a recognized
function of the civilized governments which hold
sway over uncivilized or less civilized lands.
Modern man has been educated to treat wild life
with greater restraint, and the ideals of the
modern hunter of big game are concentrated
more on the acquisition of good representative
trophies. Record heads may be his great ambition, but these must always be largely a matter of
luck. Since the perfection of photography some
men have laid aside the rifle for the camera and
no doubt this is a form of sport second to none.

Throughout the book I have made every effort
to obtain strict accuracy, and wherever any estimated figures are given I have also set forth the
data on which such estimates are based. So far
as possible I have given details of the methods of
hunting. This is important, as a bag of lions
made with the assistance of a large pack of dogs
is a very different feat to a like number killed
without such aid. I need hardly stress the
enormous advantage held by later-day hunters
armed with high-velocity breech-loading weapons
over the Nimrods of the muzzle-loading days.

Whenever I have been able to obtain it I have given particulars of the weapons used.

Though in many instances I am confident that the bags quoted are in fact actual records, it is not possible to be certain of this in every case. Many men of great experience are reticent in mentioning their achievements, and many of the old hunters have left but meagre details concerning their bags. Little did many of them realize that countries, which in their time teemed with game, would in fifty or less years be practically destitute of large animals. They could not foresee that their experiences and achievements would so soon become facts of considerable historical interest; had they done so, my task would doubtless have proved easier than has been the case. As might be expected the search for European records was easier and the details of sport in mediæval Europe afford a clear indication of the extraordinary devotion to the chase exhibited by the nobility and landed proprietors of those days.

By careful research and enquiry I have endeavoured to achieve a result in keeping with the title of the book, but I shall welcome any additional information that my readers may care to send me.

CHAPTER I

AFRICAN ELEPHANTS

ACCORDING to Professor H. Fairfield Osborn, man has been a hunter of mastodons and elephants for the sake of their bones, ivory, and flesh, for a million and a quarter years.

The question of the comparative danger of various wild beasts has always been a highly controversial subject, but, certain it is, that the pursuit of elephants is one of the most dangerous of sports, and most hunters of experience have placed the elephant either first, second or third, on the list of dangerous game.

In the early days of South Africa, when these animals were to be found in relatively open country, it was possible to pursue them on horseback, but the constant persecution to which they were subjected had the effect of driving them into the " fly " infested country of the interior where horses could no longer be used. With this principal exception the African elephant is hunted on foot, and if consistently followed up this represents the most exacting form of sport in the world.

The restrictions now placed upon elephant hunting seem to preclude the possibility of the enormous bags that follow ever being equalled, and elephant hunting as a remunerative profession is a thing of the past.

So far as I have been able to ascertain, the most successful African elephant hunter of all time is Mr. W. D. M. Bell, who has killed 983 bulls and 28 cows, making a total of 1,011 elephants.*

W. D. M. BELL

I am greatly indebted to Mr. Bell for the many intimate details concerning his career which follow.

Born in 1880, he formed the fixed intention of becoming an elephant hunter at an early age. He landed in Africa towards the end of the last century, and success attended his earliest efforts. Since that time he has spent sixteen and a half years on the actual hunting grounds and has shot in the following localities: Kenya, Karamojo, Abyssinia, Sudan, Lado Enclave, French Ivory Coast, Liberia, French Congo and Belgian Congo. All these countries contributed their quota of elephants to his enormous bag as the accompanying list shows.

* W.D.M.B. *in litt.* 23rd March 1931.

AFRICAN ELEPHANTS

Locality.	Bull Elephants.
Mombasa-Malindi Coast . .	14
Tana River	17
Masindi District . . .	23
Mount Elgon	42
Mani-Mani	91
Dodose	63
Dabossa	149
Lado Enclave	266
French Ivory Coast . . .	80
Liberia	27
French Congo	189
Belgian Congo	22
	983

With regard to these figures Mr. Bell says: " I have not included cow elephants shot for meat or in defence of myself or attendants. The number so shot is 28, making the total 1,011 ".

The largest number of bull elephants he ever shot in one day was 19. Other days yielded 17, 16, 15. on three occasions, 14 and 12 on three occasions. His best month produced 44, all killed in three consecutive days, and in his worst month he did not even see one.

His most disappointing day he describes thus: " 54 bull elephants (mostly huge) found and counted, all travelling steadily along. Got directly into path and waited until leaders bore ten and fifteen paces to front on either hand and then succeeded in dropping only 5 out of that magnificent millionaire herd. They split up in all directions and at Hell's own gait. Alas! what should I have done?" His most pleasantly memorable experience—"When my partner said: 'Well, Bell, I'm damned', after watching me from a tree-top run down and kill 6 large bulls out of 6 in long grass, at mid-day, in as many minutes".

His heaviest yield of ivory as the result of one day's shooting amounted to 1,643 lbs. of soft ivory from 11 head containing 21 tusks, one being a single tusker. The average weight was over 77 lbs. and the value £863.

The following detailed results which he has kindly given me are, I think, of exceptional interest.

Yield from five best Safaris

Weight of Ivory			Value
14,780 lbs.	.	.	. £7,300
14,247 lbs.	.	.	. 7,082
12,814 lbs.	.	.	. 6,923
11,024 lbs.	.	.	. 4,792
10,670 lbs.	.	.	. 4,230

AFRICAN ELEPHANTS

Best Year

Ivory sold	. .	. £7,300
Expenditure	.	. 3,100

Profit	£4,200

Worst Year

Expenditure	.	. £3,400
Ivory sold	. .	. 1,563

Loss	£1,837

These are wonderful figures, but the extra-ordinarly severe nature of the work may be judged from the fact that Mr. Bell informs me that his average yearly consumption of boot leather amounted to 24 pairs, and he estimates that the total mileage covered on foot, including going to and returning from hunting grounds, amounts to 73 miles for every elephant killed.

His most unpleasant experience he describes as " Travelling hot-foot 8½ hours at 6 miles per hour on enormous track in wet season to find a tuskless bull ! Killed to prevent a recurrence ! " The feet of his native assistants, carrying water bottle and spare rifle, lasted on an average for four months, at one month on and one month in the base camp. Their soles he says were then right down to the quick, in spite of sandals. One of his men alone stuck it for ten months on end, but then retired altogether. Since it may prove of interest to know some of his rules of life when engaged in this arduous work, I will quote the following from the notes he has given me: " Best method of keeping one's own feet in working condition in spite of rubs and blisters, is to wash socks every day and powder them thickly with boracic. Best diet for hunting—sour milk and dried buck meat (biltong). Next best—elephant trunk, cut small and stewed, with native vegetables and flour. Worst diet for hunting—the ingredients in what is known as doing yourself well ".

Mr. Bell has related many of his experiences in his most excellent book, " The Wanderings of an Elephant Hunter ", which was published in 1923. There is nothing more remarkable in that book than his account of a day in the Lado Enclave in which he ran a herd of elephants to a walking pace. This notable day started by his killing a white rhino with a magnificent horn; by 8 a.m. he was at the heels of the herd of elephants and at sundown, or 6 p.m., he found himself passing the carcase of the rhino he had killed in the morning, having travelled all day in an enormous circle. He had the herd well in hand by 2 p.m.

and at the finish they seemed quite incapable of anything more than a walking pace. He bagged 15 bulls from the herd, but though he often attempted to repeat the feat with other herds he was never able to live with them except for a short distance.

With regard to rifles, Mr. Bell tried many at one time and another including a double .450/.400 and magazine rifles of various calibre. He formed a very definite preference for magazine weapons and for many years used the .275 and the .256 in every kind of country and against every kind of game. His greatest successes were achieved with the 7 mm. Rigby-Mauser or .276, firing the old round-nosed solid bullet.

As a big game shot it is difficult to write regarding his skill. Most first-class men are reticent on this subject, but those who have read Mr. Bell's book, " The Wanderings of an Elephant Hunter ", will have quickly sensed the fact that it was written by a man of exceptional ability with the rifle. An exact knowledge of the anatomy of game, a rule never to fire unless he knew exactly where he was placing his bullet, and a temperament that enabled him to retain a perfect control over himself in every moment of danger or excitement were important contributory factors to his wonderful success. He invariably carried his own rifle, and the natural aptitude which he must undoubtedly have possessed, together with the years of incessant practice which his life as a hunter entailed, combined in giving him an almost complete control over his game, irrespective of the angle at which it presented a shot. For actual examples indicating his skill I am able to give two instances, but since these relate to experiences with buffaloes and lions I must refer the reader to the respective chapters devoted to these two animals. Outstanding ability with the rifle would not alone account for Mr. Bell's success; an iron constitution and a physique capable of withstanding the constant exposure and strain to which it was subjected, a thorough knowledge of the game he followed, and last, but by no means least, a complete understanding of, and ability to handle the natives, were all vital factors in his truly wonderful career.

(For further notes on W. D. M. Bell refer to Chapters III and VI.)

JAMES SUTHERLAND

One of the most successful elephant hunters in the equatorial regions of Africa was Mr. James Sutherland who killed 447 bull elephants.* He first went to South Africa, arriving at Cape Town

* The Adventures of an Elephant Hunter by James Sutherland (Preface).

in 1896, and subsequently visited Johannesburg, Mafeking, Matabeleland, Beira, Mashonaland, Lake Tanganyika and the Congo.   During this time he was engaged in various occupations, and though he states that he did some promiscuous hunting from Beira it was not until he arrived in Portuguese East Africa in 1902 that he decided to become an elephant hunter.   In 1904 he moved into what was then German East Africa, where he continued to hunt until 1912.   During these ten years he got some splendid tusks, the heaviest he mentions weighing 152 lbs. + 137½ lbs.*   In 1912 Mr. Sutherland published some of his experiences in a book entitled " The Adventures of an Elephant Hunter ".   This book is, I believe, out of print and becoming rather scarce, but in addition to recounting many of his experiences it contains some excellent notes on the natural history aspect of big game, together with some most informative reading on the native tribes and the native mind.

In the course of his hunting career Sutherland experienced some very narrow escapes.   He was twice caught by elephants and once by a buffalo. In one of the elephant incidents he was hurled into the air and fell on the animal's back; an experience probably unique of its kind.

* The Adventures of an Elephant Hunter (p. 108).

BIG GAME SHOOTING RECORDS

The occurrence of an elephant being stunned by a shot and being mistaken for dead is not altogether uncommon, but Sutherland records an instance where he actually sat on the head of a supposedly dead elephant for a short rest.   On returning to the spot some short while afterwards the animal had gone and he never saw it again.

For elephant and rhinoceros shooting Sutherland preferred a heavy rifle.   After using and experimenting with all kinds he says: " I find the most effective to be the double .577 with a 750 grains bullet and a charge in axite powder equivalent to a hundred grains of cordite ".   A single trigger, ejector weapon of this type, with hand detachable locks, that was built by Messrs. Westley Richards & Co., gave him every satisfaction and contributed largely in the making of his great bag.   It is probable that his bag of elephants is now considerably in excess of the figure I have quoted, but I have been unable to obtain particulars as he is I believe at the present time somewhere in the Congo.

ARTHUR H. NEUMANN

For some reason or other A. H. Neumann has frequently been credited with shooting a far greater number of elephants than was actually the case. The probable explanation of the misconception is as follows. Neumann spent the greater part of his life in Africa and being a man of an exceedingly retiring and sensitive nature his movements and achievements were known to only a few people. He was one of the earliest elephant hunters in East Africa, and when in 1897 he published his book, " Elephant Hunting in East Equatorial Africa ", which deals most fully with his experiences over a period of three years, he became established in the eyes of the public as an elephant hunter and nothing more, whereas, as a matter of actual fact, he was 43 years of age and had spent the greater part of twenty-four years in Africa before he organized his first expedition after elephants. Following the publication of his book, the world at large learnt nothing more from his own pen regarding the rest of his life and practically nothing from other sources. After his death his great friend, Mr. J. G. Millais, wrote some interesting notes on his life which were published in his book " Wanderings and Memories ". Meanwhile, his fame as an elephant hunter had spread and, as is sometimes the case, it was more on account of what was surmised rather than on what was actually known that he came to be credited with a bag far in excess of what he actually shot. That Neumann was a skilful and highly successful elephant hunter is an undoubted fact, but that he killed the great number of elephants that have sometimes been attributed to him is quite erroneous. The exact number that he did shoot I have been unable to ascertain, but it is possible to form a very close estimate as I shall presently show. The one man that I thought might know the actual figure was Mr. J. G. Millais, but in September, 1930, he informed me that he himself did not know and that he did not think the information was obtainable from any other source.

Born at Hockley Rectory in Bedfordshire in June, 1850, Neumann landed in South Africa in 1869 and until 1876 was variously employed in coffee planting, cotton and tobacco cultivation, gold digging, and running a trading post in Swaziland. From 1877 till the Zulu War in 1879 (in which he was made captain) he was mainly engaged in shooting in the Transvaal and Swaziland, and from 1880 to 1887 with shooting and travelling on the Limpopo and Sabi Rivers. Of this period of his life we know little, but in writing about it in his book he states that he shot much game in South-eastern Africa and of most kinds peculiar to the country with the notable exception

28

of elephants. It is clear from his writings that he had some intention of one day writing about his South African experiences, but unfortunately he never did so.

It was not until 1890, when he entered the East Africa Company and was engaged in exploration for the rail route, that he shot his first elephant. In 1892 he became a magistrate in Zululand, but not caring for the work he decided to return to East Africa and organize his first elephant hunting expedition. Arriving at Mombasa in 1893 he devoted the three following years to hunting and wandering in the far interior amongst the Ndorobo savages in the neighbourhood of Mount Kenia and the Lorogi Mountains. He penetrated north to Lake Rudolph and while hunting from Bumi, where he enjoyed some splendid sport, he was seriously injured by a cow elephant. The .303 which he was using missed fire and the cow knocked him down and crushed in his ribs. He was carefully tended by the natives and lived on milk for weeks, but it was two months before he could lie in any position except on his back. In connection with his trip to Lake Rudolph, Millais says that it was a great disappointment to him to find on his return to Mombasa that Count Teleki had already described the lake, of which Neumann himself thought he was the discoverer.* I do not think this is correct as Neumann's book seems to indicate quite clearly that not only did he know of the existence and name of the lake, but one of his followers had actually been with Teleki at the time of its discovery. It is this period, 1893-1896, which his book covers, and since every elephant incident during this time is fully described, a careful perusal of it will show that he shot 69 elephants in these three years.

Towards the end of 1896 he came home, and in 1897 his very fine book was published by Messrs. Rowland Ward. It is one of the best works that has ever been written on the subject of elephant hunting, but, unfortunately, it is now decidedly scarce and a good copy commands from five to seven times its published price.

From this point we depend on Mr. J. G. Millais for the details of the remainder of his life.

In November, 1899, he went to South Africa to take part in the Boer War and he had a very narrow escape at Spion Kop, a bullet going through his hat and passing through his hair. He entered Ladysmith with the relief force and at the end of hostilities came home.

It was not until early in 1902 that he returned to East Africa and went into the Mount Kenia

* "Wanderings and Memories ": 1919: p. 143.

country. He was successful in his hunting, and in March, 1903, when he came down to Mombasa he brought with him over a ton of ivory. Now even allowing for the fact that some of the ivory was small, a ton would hardly represent more than sixty tusks, so that his bag for this period was probably round about 30 elephants. After refitting he continued hunting in the regions of Turkana, Northern Gwaso Nyiro, the Lorian Swamp and Turkwel until July, 1906, and the yield from these years was ivory worth £4,500.* Now if we take this sum as representing 9,000 lbs. of ivory and the average weight of the tusks as being 100 lbs. the pair, it equals a bag of 90 elephants. In October, 1906, he arrived home again and he died in London in 1907.

From the foregoing it will be seen that he devoted about seven years to elephant hunting, and allowing for the fact that he kept some of his best tusks as specimens, and that he killed a few elephants when in the service of the East African Company, he may have killed 200 elephants.

I have dealt with this matter at some length as it is a subject about which such varying views have been expressed.

Neumann enjoyed some splendid days, getting 14 elephants on one day, 12 and a black

* " Wanderings and Memories " : 1919 : p. 156.

rhinoceros with a 40 in. horn on another and 10 elephants on another. That he was a fine shot admits of no doubt. On the day in which he shot the 12 elephants and 1 rhino his expenditure of cartridges was only 20, and on another occasion in the Lorian Swamp he scored a double right and left at bull elephants. I have seen his day's bag for the former occasion quoted as 11 elephants and a rhino, but though it is true that one of the dead elephants was not found the same day, the ivory from all twelve was eventually recovered.

In the course of his career he got some good though not remarkable tusks; the best he mentions being 117½ lbs. + 109 lbs., and he got a good many others of nearly equal weight. The longest but not heaviest bull tusk of which I can find information measured 9 ft. 5 in. and his best cow tusks were a remarkably fine pair weighing 38 lbs. + 39 lbs.

From 1893 till 1902 Neumann shot most of his elephants with a double .577 by Gibbs and a .303 service Lee-Metford. He also tried a double 10-bore which he acquired to take the place of one of his other weapons that was damaged, but he did not like it. In 1902 he acquired a double .450 by Rigby which suited him exactly.

In the later years of his life he cared but little for most forms of shooting, but of the elephant he says: " Him I worship—I have become a true Ndorobo in that ".

He was a keen student of natural history and he also accomplished valuable work in Africa apart from the years he devoted to hunting. Wherever he went he won the respect and admiration of the natives as those following in his footsteps were quick to appreciate.

PETRUS JACOBS

Of the early Boer hunters in South Africa, Petrus Jacobs seems without doubt to have been the most famous, and no less an authority than F. C. Selous has described him as " the most experienced elephant-hunter in South Africa ".[*]

Jacobs must have been born somewhere about the year 1800 since he was over seventy-three years of age when Selous met him. At that time he was still actively employed, and just as keen on hunting as he had always been. Unlike many Boers, he loved the hunting of dangerous game for its own sake, and never declined the opportunity of attacking a lion. Most of his hunting was done from horseback, but at quite an advanced age he hunted in the " fly " country and killed many elephants on foot. The exact num-

[*] " A Hunter's Wanderings in Africa."

ber he shot we do not know but he is believed to have killed between 400 and 500 bull elephants.[*]

Some further notes on this remarkable old man in connection with his lion hunting experiences occur in Chapter VI.

WILLIAM FINAUGHTY

William Finaughty was the greatest English elephant hunter in South Africa and it is somewhat curious that those who were contemporary with him should not have given more information about his life. Selous mentions him, but does not go into details, and it was left to an American gentleman in the person of Mr. G. L. Harrison to repair the omission.

Mr. Harrison met Finaughty in 1913 and though he was then a very slight old man and weakened by fever, he still retained a wonderful memory, and his friends told Mr. Harrison that he was still a wonderful shot with either rifle or gun. Finaughty gave Harrison the numbers of the " Rhodesian Journal " containing his hunting experiences. One or two of the numbers were missing, but as the Journal had gone out of existence they could not be replaced.

Finaughty was one of the first white men to

[*] J. G. Millais : " The Life of F. C. Selous " : 1918 : p. 75.

hunt elephants in Matabeleland and Mr. Harrison was so impressed by his reminiscences that on his return to America he had them reproduced in book form under the title of " The Recollections of William Finaughty—Elephant Hunter, 1864-1875 ". Two hundred and fifty copies of this most excellent little volume were privately printed, and this I think is our only source of information concerning the adventurous life of this great hunter.

At the age of 21, Finaughty left Grahamstown early in 1864 and travelled north through the Free State, the plains of which then teemed with game. Concerning this wonderful country he says : " I could never have believed that such a quantity of wild animals would congregate together. As far as the eye could see it was one moving mass, tens of thousands of beautiful wild creatures of many kinds, consisting for the most part of black wildebeest, blesbok, springbok, a sprinkling of ostrich, quagga, and blue wildebeest ".

In due course he entered Matabeleland and eventually reached Tati. At this time Mzilikatse was the chief of the Matabele and he treated Finaughty and his party in a friendly manner. This was Finaughty's first introduction to the Matabele and he saw their famous army in its prime. He was present at a dance of about 25,000 warriors in their war dress, and in connection with this great function no less than 540 oxen were killed. Finaughty shot his first two elephants on this trip but his party lost fourteen horses out of seventeen owing to horse sickness. In 1865 and 1866 he made two expeditions on his own account with the principal object of trading, but he shot a few elephants and in 1867 he decided to become a professional hunter. From this date till 1876 the greater part of his time was devoted to hunting, though he gave it up at one period to give himself a rest from the arduous life. He established a large store and for a time carried on a profitable business but he returned to the hunter's life.

The exact number of elephants he killed in his lifetime we do not know, but from a careful perusal of his " Recollections " it is clear that he shot over 400. In one year he shot 111 elephants yielding 5,000 lbs. of ivory. On the Umbila he met with great success and it is probable that the elephants in this part of the country had never heard a shot fired before as on one occasion he bagged 6 bulls in a river bed without their showing alarm at the shots. His record bag for one day was 10, 5 bulls and 5 cows. Nearly all his hunting was done on horseback and he was without doubt a fine horseman and a splendid shot. On one occasion with only five bullets with him he came upon elephants unexpectedly. He shot 5 elephants with his five bullets and on examining one which he had shot at close quarters he found the bullet lodged under the skin on the far side. He promptly cut this out and with it bagged a sixth elephant, thus performing the unique feat of getting 6 elephants with only five bullets. The heaviest pair of tusks he ever got weighed 250 lbs.

Most of his shooting was done with an old muzzle-loader firing a 4 oz. bullet propelled by a handful of black powder, the recoil from which made it difficult for him to keep his seat in the saddle. In 1876 he used breech-loading weapons for the first time, but he found a 12-bore firing home-made and heavily-loaded cartridges terribly punishing in its recoil so he then tried a light Westley Richards fall block rifle of which he says: " This was my first experience of a small, but really effective, breech-loader without a bad recoil to it. It delighted me and I quickly profited by it ". On his first day with it he shot 1 bull and 6 cow elephants, and he says: " It was a revelation to me as to what could be done with a small gun after my long experience with a large elephant gun ".

BIG GAME SHOOTING RECORDS

This was his last year's serious shooting, but so profitable had been his hunting and trading that he was able to face his remaining years with equanimity. From 1883 to 1887 he lived in the Traansvaal and then following a few years spent in Johannesburg he retired to his farm near Bulawayo.

ROUALEYN GORDON CUMMING

Gordon Cumming hunted in South Africa between the years 1843 and 1848 and during this period he killed 105 elephants.* Few hunters gained a greater notoriety than he, but looking back on his life at this distance of time we are able to review his career in better perspective than was possible to the public who first read the account of his experiences.

His book, " Five Years of a Hunter's Life in South Africa ", was first published in 1850 and it quickly gave rise to much discussion, and doubts were sometimes expressed as to the accuracy of some of the incidents described. Since that time the book has run through a large number of editions and has probably been as widely read as any book of its kind. Written in a somewhat romantic style, page after page recounts the de-

* " Five Years of a Hunter's Life in South Africa."

tails of what he killed, and this is probably the reason for the not uncommonly expressed opinion that he shot an enormous and unsportsmanlike quantity of game. As a matter of actual fact there is no real reason for thinking that he killed more than many of his contemporaries and it is probable that he actually shot less. If, as is the case in his book, the account of a great deal of shooting over a period of five years is compressed into a few hundred pages and then read through in the matter of a few hours, it is very liable to convey a wrong impression. With the exception of his bag of elephants we have not any other exact figures of the game that he did kill, but the following are the largest bags for individual days mentioned in his book : —

14 Springboks in one day.
1 Springbock, 3 Wildebeests, 1 Hartebeest,
    1 Blesbok in one day.
7 Hippopotami in one day.
5 Buffaloes in one day.
1 Elephant and 4 Rhinoceros in one night.
4 Elephants in one night.

The 14 springboks were shot from countless thousands on migration, where the number could easily have been doubled or trebled. Now there is nothing very extravagant about these figures for Africa, where the native ever looks to the white man for a supply of meat. Of Gordon Cumming, Mr. Millais has written as follows: "from all accounts, gathered from independent sources, it is now admitted that Gordon Cumming was a fearless hunter and did in the main accomplish all the principal exploits to which he laid claim".

Born on the 15th March, 1820, he was the second son of Sir William G. Gordon Cumming, Bart., of Altyre, and in his early life roe-deer stalking and salmon fishing were his chief amusements. In 1839 he sailed for India to join his regiment, the 4th Madras Light Cavalry, and touching at the Cape *en route* he had the opportunity of hunting some of the smaller antelopes. In India he obtained some sport and added considerably to his natural history collection, but the climate did not suit him so he retired from the service and returned home. In Scotland deer-stalking satisfied him for a time, but with a view to obtaining sport in the far West he obtained a commission in the Royal Veteran Newfoundland Companies. The chances of sport did not materialize, however, so he effected an exchange into the Cape Riflemen and in 1843 was again in South Africa. Once again he was disappointed in his expectation of finding opportunities for

* " The Life of F. C. Selous " : 1918 : p. 66.

shooting, so he decided to sell out of the Army and devote his time to hunting and collecting.

On the 23rd October, 1843, he started on his first expedition, and five years later on the completion of his fifth and last trip into the interior he returned home.

An exhibition of all his African trophies was held in London at 232, Piccadilly, and afterwards they were removed to Scotland. Following his death at Fort Augustus on the 24th March, 1866, at the early age of 46, the collection was purchased by Barnum the showman, but unfortunately it was, I believe, completely destroyed in his great fire.

Of the many tales of fact and fiction concerning his deer-stalking escapades I do not intend to write, but for a pen picture of the man I am tempted to quote that brilliant essayist, Mr. Patrick R. Chalmers: " to fall in with Roualyn in some dark and forbidden corrie must have been a romantic thing and a little awesome. Out of the mist would stride a great, eagle-beaked, kilted fellow—six-foot-four stood Roualyn. His hair fell to his broad shoulders, his beard to his slim waist. He wore a flat grey bonnet, he carried a rifle and, over his back, was swung a spy-glass and, maybe, the head of a royal—for Roualyn took the hill without ghillies and left his venison for the ravens or the shepherd who might choose to fetch it and tell him of more ".

Of Gordon Cumming's ability as an elephant hunter it is not easy to speak. Most of his shooting was done on horseback with the assistance of dogs to distract the animal's attention and some he killed at night by waiting at their drinking places. Judging by his writings he must have been a pretty good shot at most kinds of game, and though he sometimes seems to have been tempted to fire at excessive ranges. he usually strove to get to close quarters with elephants. The number of shots however that he sometimes expended before he was able to finish a bull elephant was certainly enormous and on this account he was rarely able to bag more than one animal out of a herd. The following are striking examples of the gladiatorial nature of some of his encounters: " I fought one of the former (an elephant) in dense wait-a-bit jungle from half-past eleven till the sun was under, when his tough old spirit fled, and he fell pierced with fifty-seven balls ", or again: " I was therefore obliged to hunt him on foot, and slew him with thirty bullets, after an extremely severe and dangerous combat of about two hours ", or yet again: " In the afternoon I was engaged for three to four hours combating with a vicious elephant which I finished with thirty-five bullets in the shoulder, in an impracticable jungle of wait-a-bit thorns ".

On some occasions, of course, he accounted for his game more quickly, but the probability is that his weapons lacked penetrative power. Concerning his battery in Africa he mentions three double-barrelled rifles by Purdey, William Moore, and Dickson of Edinburgh; a single-barrelled 12-bore of German manufacture, a double rifle with spare shot barrels by Westley Richards and a 4-bore, all of course being muzzle-loaders. We do not know their respective charges of powder but two of his weapons burst. Armed as he was, a bag of 105 elephants must have represented an enormous amount of hard and hazardous work.

According to "O Benguella" of 6th March, 1909, the professional Danish hunter, Karl Larsen, had, at that date, killed over 300 elephants. He had then spent seventeen years hunting and collecting in West and East Africa and during the latter part of this period he used a double-barrelled .600 by W. J. Jeffery & Co. Ltd. for the hunting of elephants and other dangerous game.

Of the Boer elephant hunters, Jan Viljoen had a great reputation and he continued hunting on foot in the " fly " country after many of his contemporaries had given up the game for good. It was the custom of the Boer hunters to travel into the interior with their wives, children, stock, etc., and establish a standing camp which acted as a base for the actual hunting expeditions. On the authority of William Finaughty it can be stated that in 1867 Viljoen and his party shot 210 elephants, and this probably constitutes the record bag of elephants made in a single season by one hunting party.

About the year 1878 there occurred in the region of the upper Okavango the greatest and most wanton butchery of elephants known in the history of South Africa. The Van Zyls's and some other Dutch hunters drove a herd of 104 elephants into a deep morass where they were helpless and before the end of the day every one had been killed irrespective of sex or size.* Referring to this day Mr. H. A. Bryden has said that " there were few with good tusks and the slaughter seems to have been as unprofitable as it was unpardonable.

Of the English hunters in South Africa no name is more widely known or respected than that of F. C. Selous, but though his long and distinguished African career started with the hunting of elephants as a profession, his fame as a hunter probably rests more on the fact that he acquired

* " Gun and Camera in Southern Africa " : p. 489.

the finest collection of South African trophies ever shot by one man. For this reason I have thought it more appropriate to deal with his achievements as a hunter under the heading of " Other African Game Animals ", though here it may be stated that he shot 106 elephants in the course of his lifetime.

Other English hunters with a considerable experience of elephant hunting in South Africa included Capt. (afterwards Sir) Cornwallis Harris, William Cotton Oswell (referred to at greater length in Chapter V) and William Charles Baldwin, all of whom wrote valuable accounts of their travels and experiences.

Of the many successful men in the Equatorial regions of Africa the names of Major C. H. Stigand and T. A. Barns may be mentioned. Major Stigand was badly mauled at one time and another by an elephant, a lion and a rhinoceros, and he was eventually killed when engaged on a punitive expedition against a native tribe. Barns will always be remembered as the man who shot the great bull elephant which is now preserved for the nation in the Natural History Museum in London.

All these men shot a considerable number of elephants but not in numbers to equal the bags mentioned in the earlier pages of this chapter.

CHAPTER II

ASIATIC ELEPHANTS

FOR countless generations the Indian elephant has been caught and domesticated and there is little evidence that their numbers in a wild state have fluctuated in India to anything like the same extent as in Ceylon.   In some parts of India they have at times been sufficiently numerous for a reward to be offered for their destruction and as much as £7 per head was once paid by the Madras Government.   At the time, native hunters armed with small cannon mounted on tripods, which fired half-pound balls, are said to have sometimes killed as many as five or six in a day.*   The value attaching to the domesticated animal however, and measures of protection, have resulted in their numbers being reasonably well maintained.   I do not think bags in any way comparable with those of Ceylon have ever been made in India.   G. P. Sanderson, author of "Thirteen Years among the Wild Beasts of India", killed no more than " about twenty ", but in Ceylon they formerly existed in enormous num-

* " Thirteen Years among the Wild Beasts of India."

46

bers and rewards for their destruction of 7/- or 10/- were in force for a considerable time. Ceylon elephants are usually tuskless; an adult bull stands about 9 ft. at the shoulder and they are more easily killed than African elephants.

So far as I have been able to ascertain the record bag of elephants for Ceylon was made by Major Rogers, who is believed to have killed about 1,500.

Before proceeding to discuss this statement and other figures I must point out that all the big bags of Ceylon elephants were made about a hundred years ago and it is therefore impossible to obtain first-hand information concerning them.

In "The Field" of 22nd September, 1894, under the heading of "Largest bag of elephants made in Ceylon", there occurred the following letter, written by E. L. Layard of Otterbourne, Budleigh Salterton: "'A. Fogey' in his gossip about the .303 rifle, etc. (p. 338, No. 2175, Sept. 1) says the largest bag of elephants ever made by one man in Ceylon (numbering over 300) was made by a gentleman who did all his slaughter with a 16 smooth bore. If 'A. Fogey' means that they were killed in one day, I know nothing of it; but if he means the bag to represent the total number killed by one man he is sadly under the mark. The numbers killed by the old elephant hunters (most of them now dead and gone) far exceeded this. Major Rogers killed over 1,500, Capt. Gallwey 1,300, Capt. Skinner 1,200, Capt. Layard 1,000, and many others of later days, such as the brothers Baker, made nearly as large bags. Major Rogers always used 16-bores, cut down to 20 or 22 inches in length. I had one of his amputated guns. It was only fit for ball, would not throw shot with any effect. Most of the old hunters used small (16) smooth bores ".

It will be noted that Capt. Layard, who is mentioned as having shot 1,000 elephants, and the writer of the foregoing letter bear the same name, so it is reasonable to suppose that they were related and that E. L. Layard wrote with full knowledge of the facts, but some of the bags he mentions differ from those quoted by Harry Storey in his excellent book " Hunting and Shooting in Ceylon " (1907). From this work I take the following: " After 1831 the destruction of elephants was encouraged owing to their depredations and numbers, and Major Forbes mentions the killing of 106 elephants in 1837 by a party of four Europeans in three days . . . . . Coming to later times, in the 'forties Major Rogers is credited with having slain upwards of 1,400; Captain Gallwey over 700; and Major Skinner, ' the roadmaker ', almost as many ".

ASIATIC ELEPHANTS

If we turn to the writings of that other great authority on Ceylon sport, Sir Samuel W. Baker, we find that though he mentions both Major Rogers and Captain Gallwey he gives no information concerning their bags. I have been unable to trace any other references to these men and their exploits.

With regard to Sir Samuel W. Baker's own bag, his exact figures for elephants are unknown, but on page 86, Vol. I, of his book, " Wild Beasts and their Ways ", he says: " I have killed some hundreds in my early life ".

What the record individual bag for a single day's shooting may have been I do not know, but Major Forbes writing in 1840 states that " fifteen wild elephants were actually docked by a gentleman in one forenoon. The tail of the elephant, like the brush of a fox, is the signal of success ".*

A collective bag of great magnitude is mentioned by Sir Samuel W. Baker. Writing in 1855, he says: †"Although the number of these animals is still so immense in Ceylon, they must nevertheless have been much reduced within the last twenty years. In those days the country was overrun with them, and some idea of their numbers may be gathered from the fact that three

* " Eleven Years in Ceylon " : 1840 : Vol. I : p. 288.
† " Eight Years' Wanderings in Ceylon " : 1855 : p. 127.

first-rate shots in three days bagged 104 elephants. This was told me by one of the parties concerned, and it throws our modern shooting into the shade ".

I have already stated that we do not know the exact number of elephants that Sir Samuel Baker shot, but since his name is so closely identified with Ceylon and its elephants, this seems the most appropriate place to say something about his remarkable career.

SIR SAMUEL W. BAKER

Sir Samuel Baker's chief claim to fame and the grateful remembrance of his country rests on more than his big game hunting exploits. As an explorer, administrator and publicist he accomplished much, but this aspect of his life has already been fully and ably dealt with in the memoir written by T. Douglas Murray and A. Silva White. As a hunter, his experience of practically all the dangerous game animals is probably unrivalled.

Born in London on the 8th June, 1821, he spent many of his early years at Highnam Court, and on some 2,000 acres of surrounding land he first learnt to shoot. Following a couple of years in the Mauritus he decided to go to Ceylon in order to satisfy his craving to taste wild sports in a wild country.   He arrived in that island in 1846 and subsequently enjoyed every form of sport that the country afforded.   On the completion of this first trip he came home, but he was so fascinated with the life and the country that he decided to return and settle in the beautiful and healthy district of Newera Ellia.   During the eight years that he remained in Ceylon he engaged in elephant and buffalo shooting, deer-stalking, hunting the sambar and wild boar with his own hounds and the hunting knife, and coursing the axis deer with greyhounds.   He wrote some splendid accounts of his experiences in all these sports in his stirring and full-blooded book " The Rifle and Hound in Ceylon ".

If elephants were not as numerous in Baker's time as they had once been, they still existed in very great numbers and, as has already been stated, he shot some hundreds of these animals. They were usually found in dense jungle or high lemon-grass which made it necessary to get within about ten paces in order to obtain a shot at the brain.   For this class of work Baker usually employed three double 10-bore rifles (muzzle-loaders) and, when once a herd had been attacked, much of the subsequent success depended on the skill and staunchness of the gun bearers in handling the spare rifles. A stern end-on chase usually followed the first shots, and an enormous effort was required to keep touch with the flying herd and to gain positions from which further vital shots could be attempted. There are many such hunts described in " The Rifle and Hound in Ceylon " and that Baker was a first-class shot is apparent. On the 1st December, 1851, he bagged 6 out of 6 fired at, and there are many other instances recorded which illustrate his skill and endurance. On one occasion he was caught by a bull elephant which struck him on the thigh with its tusk and hurled him a distance of eight or ten paces. The beast then proceeded to beat the grass with its trunk in search of its victim. The animal's acute power of scent how-ever had probably been momentarily spoiled by the powder and smoke of the shot Baker had fired when the beast was all but upon him. However this may be, the elephant eventually abandoned his search and Baker was lucky to have escaped without even a broken bone. Had he not jumped aside after firing he would probably have been struck in the stomach instead of the thigh, and then the result might well have been different.

A sport of which he never tired was the hunt-ing of the solitary old rogue elephants which frequently inhabited the vicinity of tanks or reservoirs. During his first year in Ceylon he was armed with two single-barrelled muzzle-loaders and, though these were weapons of great power, there was no room for error in the pursuit of such dangerous game. The use of these rifles, however, taught him to rely on his first shot and gave him absolute confidence in his own powers. In the neighbourhood of Monampitya he once killed an immense tank rogue with a single shot in the temple. This was by far the largest elephant he ever saw in Ceylon, and of quite exceptional dimensions for that country. Describing its appearance when alive, he says: "although his head and carcase were enormous, still his length of leg appeared disproportionately great"—and when dead—" His height may be imagined from this rough method of measuring. A gun-bearer climbed upon his back as the elephant lay upon all fours, and holding a long stick across his spine at right angles, I could just touch it with the points of my fingers by reaching to my utmost height. Thus, as he lay, his back was seven feet two inches, perpendicular height, from the ground. This would make his height, when erect, about twelve feet on the spine—an enormous height for an elephant, as twelve feet on the top of the back is about equal to eleven feet six inches at the shoulder ".

Other kinds of game abounded in various parts of the island. Of the axis deer, he says: " In the neighbourhood of Paliar, and Illepecadéivé on the north-west coast, I have shot them till I was satiated, and it ceased to be sport ". Writing of the same animal in " Wild Beasts and their Ways " he mentions having had nine bucks hanging up in camp as the produce of a single day's sport.

His buffalo shooting experiences are dealt with in the chapter devoted to that animal, but mention must here be made of the wonderful hunting he enjoyed with his powerful pack of hounds. Hunting entirely on foot, with his hunting knife as the only support for the dogs, he killed approximately 400 sambur* and a large number of wild boars, though the latter were never deliberately sought for owing to the heavy casualties they inflicted on the pack.

In 1855 Baker left Ceylon and the next year found him in Constantinople. Following a period at home in which he enjoyed some shooting and fishing in Scotland he returned to the near East in 1859 and for a couple of years was engaged in the construction of the railway across the Dobruja. During this period, with the exception of some wild-fowl shooting and some fishing, he

* " Wild Beasts and their Ways " : 1890 : Vol. II : p. 296.

had few opportunities for sport, but on the completion of this work he went to Asia Minor where he shot wild boar, roe-deer, woodcock, etc.

At this period of his life his thoughts constantly turned to Africa. The big game of that country and the mystery of the Nile sources fascinated him and he quickly decided to direct his attention to these matters.

He arrived in Africa in 1861 and during that and the following year devoted himself to exploring the Abyssinian water-ways and to big game hunting. Between 1863 and 1865 he was engaged in his epic journey of exploration which led to his discovery of the Albert N'Yanza, and such shooting as he obtained was incidental to the main object of the expedition. From 1865 to 1869 he was at home. Baker was always a keen deer-stalker, and in 1868 as the guest of the Duke of Sutherland and Lord Middleton he killed 13 stags out of 14 fired at. In 1869 he returned to Africa to take command of the historical expedition against the slave traders of the interior. This great undertaking kept him in Africa till 1873. The whole history of these wonderful years in Africa is to be found in his own books: " The Nile Tributaries of Abyssinia ", " The Albert N'Yanza " and " Ismailia ", and the results of his labours are too well known to call for comment.

BIG GAME SHOOTING RECORDS

With regard to his bag in Africa I had hoped that it might be possible to obtain fuller details than his own books give, but there are no game diaries in existence.* It would seem that he shot about 50 elephants in Africa, since on page 276 of "The Albert N'Yanza" he says that he has "measured certainly a hundred bull tusks, and . . . found them buried in the head a depth of twenty-four inches". In later years he had a good deal of experience of the domesticated elephants in India and he then declared that he would never again shoot at an elephant unless it was a dangerous rogue. On his most successful day with African elephants he killed 5, and his various writings show that his total bag in Africa included rhinoceroses, hippopotami, buffaloes, lions, giraffes, some 13 varieties of antelopes and gazelles, waterbuck, 1 wild ass, 1 ostrich, crocodiles, etc.

Between 1873 and 1879 Baker remained in England, but in the latter year he started on a trip round the world which lasted about three years. He tested the sporting capabilities of most of the countries he visited and in North America he got some splendid wapiti, bears and a bison, in addition to other game. His best wapiti head measured 59¾ inches in length and was 13 inches round the burr, whilst another fine 14-pointer was 53 inches in length, 52 inches from tip to tip, and 12½ inches round the burr.

On the completion of his world tour he settled down at his home "Sandford Orleigh". Here he usually spent the spring and summer, but the winter months were generally spent in India or Egypt. In the course of his many visits to the Central Provinces he shot 22 tigers and every one that he fired at he bagged.* He also shot considerable numbers of leopards, sloth-bears, sambur, swamp-deer, blackbuck and other Indian game.

When at home he enjoyed a certain amount of shooting. On the 17th November, 1893, he was thus employed, but this day's sport proved to be his last and on the 30th December he died.

Rather under six feet in height, Baker was a man of tremendous strength and endowed with a magnificent constitution. No man of his time can have been more powerfully armed for the pursuit of dangerous game, and his views on fire-arms were in advance of his time. When he first went to Ceylon smooth-bores of 12- or 16-gauge were commonly used for elephant hunting, but his ideas as to suitable weapons were very different. For his first trip he had built a single-

* " Sir Samuel Baker—A Memoir " : p. 399.

barrelled rifle weighing 21 lbs. firing a 3 oz. spherical ball or a 4 oz. conical projectile propelled by from 12 to 16 drams of powder which was regarded as an enormous charge in that country. He was convinced of the superiority of the rifled-barrel over the smooth-bore for all classes of work, and in the comparative weights of propellant and projectile he was aiming at a rifle on the lines of the future " Express ".

For African elephants, Messrs. Holland & Holland made for him what are probably the most powerful sporting rifles that have ever been built. These enormous weapons were single-barrelled, weighed 20 lbs., and fired a half-pound explosive shell containing a bursting charge of half an ounce propelled by 12 drams of powder. Regarding the first of these rifles Baker says: " I very seldom fired it, but it is a curious fact that I never fired a shot with that rifle without bagging; the entire practice, during several years, was confined to about 20 shots ".

Such pieces can hardly be classed as sporting weapons. though doubtless for body shots at elephants they were immensely effective and the explosive nature of the projectile would allow for a margin of error in aim. On page 200 of " Ismailia " Baker describes them as: " the most overpowering rifles I ever used. They were certain to kill the elephants and to half kill the man who fired them with 12 drachms of fine-grain powder. I was tolerably strong, therefore I was never killed outright; but an Arab hunter had his collar-bone smashed by the recoil when the rifle was loaded with simple coarse-grain powder. If he had used fine-grain, I should hardly have insured his life ".

From Baker's various writings I have carefully compiled the following list of weapons that he owned and used at one time and another as such a battery deserves to be chronicled : —

[List of Weapons follows]

Number of Weapons	Bore	Single or Double	Rifled or Smooth	Maker	Weight	Weight of Charge
1	Firing 3 oz spherical or 4 oz conical bullets — 8	Single	Rifled Two-grooved	Gibbs of Bristol	21 lbs.	12 to 16 drams
1	8	Single	Rifled Many-grooved	Blisset	16 lbs	6 drams
4	10	Double	Rifled Two-grooved	J Beattie	15 lbs.	6 drams
1	24	Double	Rifled	Fletcher of Gloucester	—	—
1	10	Double	Rifled	Latham	—	—
2	10	Double	Rifled	Reilly	14 lbs	7 drams
1	10	Double	Smooth	Beattie	—	—
1	8	Single	Rifled	Manton	—	—
1	14	Single	Rifled	Beattie	—	—
2	8	—	Rifled	Reilly	(Breech loaders)	—
2	Firing 8 oz shells	Single	Rifled	Holland & Holland	20 lbs.	12 drams
1	.577 (Express)	Double	Rifle	Holland & Holland	12 lbs (Deer-stalking rifle)	6 drams
1	360	—	Rifled	Purdey	—	—
1	Paradox ball and shot gun	—	Rifle	—	(For blackbuck etc)	—

and
various 12-bore game guns

CHAPTER III

AFRICAN BUFFALOES

THE buffaloes of the African continent are generally looked upon as being amongst the most dangerous animals of the chase. From this point of view the Cape buffalo and the bush cow of West Africa can be regarded as much the same beast. Hunters of wide experience differ in their opinions as to the comparative danger attaching to the hunting of this and other game, but William Finaughty, Sir Frederick Jackson and William Judd, have all expressed the opinion that it is the most dangerous of all African animals. Finaughty has said of the buffalo that it is " the fiercest and most cunning animal to be found in Africa. A man who is out after buffalo must shoot to kill and not to wound, and if he fails to bring his quarry down he should on no account venture to follow up unless in open country ". In considering this opinion it must be remembered that Finaughty's experience was gained in the muzzle-loading days, but Sir Frederick Jackson and William Judd are both hunters of wide experience of a much later date.

BIG GAME SHOOTING RECORDS

F. C. Selous has said: "as regards viciousness I should be inclined to put the buffalo third on the list", and W. D. M. Bell who has shot them in East, West and Central Africa has described them as "worthy game in thick stuff but ludicrously easy things to kill in open country".

Mr. W. D. M. Bell, whose opinion of the buffalo I have already quoted, has probably shot more of these animals than any other man. In the course of his career as a hunter he has killed between 600 and 700.

In connection with the above I will now quote from information that Mr. Bell has kindly supplied me with: *"In parts they (buffaloes) were the regular ration for the camp. I remember killing 23 out of 23 with a high velocity .22 rifle partly to see how effective the tiny 80 grain bullet was but chiefly because meat was required. I must have killed between six and seven hundred of these animals in all. Their hide was a constant trade article. Cut into sandal and shield sizes they never failed to attract an abundant supply of flour".

Lest the novice or moderate shot should be encouraged by the above statement to attack the dangerous game of Africa with a .22 rifle, I feel

* W.D.M.B. in litt. 23rd March 1931.

it should be stated that Mr. Bell is probably one of the most brilliant big-game shots that has ever lived. The high velocity .22 rifle in the hands of such an expert may well be an adequate weapon, but it is usually regarded as in the extreme of small bores for use against dangerous game.

As Mr. Bell was primarily an elephant hunter, fuller details of his career are to be found in Chapter I, but by way of comment on his bag of buffaloes, it can again be said that he spent sixteen and a half years on the actual hunting grounds, and, as his reputation spread and increased among the native tribes, his camp following grew in proportion. The bag is certainly enormous, but it must be remembered that the hungry mouths often numbered hundreds and it was vital to him to obtain and maintain the good-will of the natives in the many remote parts where he penetrated.

It is probable that other professional hunters in East and Central Africa have made large bags of these animals though I think it is unlikely that any of them approach Bell's figures. Great numbers must also have been shot by "skin-hunters" in South Africa before the rinderpest of 1896-7 practically wiped out the great herds. A few years prior to 1893 a Free State Boer named Montgomery, who was shooting for hides at the

Umfuli River in Mashunaland, killed 16 buffaloes out of one herd with a .450 Martini-Henry rifle.*

F. C. Selous shot 175 buffaloes† during his many years in South Africa and he subsequently shot a couple of fine specimens in East Africa. On the 20th August, 1879, when shooting for meat he killed 6 bulls with ten shots from a single-barrelled 10-bore rifle, using spherical bullets and six drachms of powder.‡ He had several very close shaves with these brutes. On one occasion in 1879 on the Chobe, he had wounded an old bull and was following it up through open bush when it charged from its concealed position from a distance of not more than ten yards. Firing from his hip he immediately sprang to one side and this probably saved him, though some part of the buffalo struck his thigh with sufficient force to throw him down. The beast's hind-leg was however broken and Selous was able to despatch him with a bullet through the lungs.

What was probably his most extraordinary experience with a buffalo occurred on the Nata River in May, 1874. He was pursuing two bulls and had twice been offered easy shots, but on both occasions his rifle had missed fire. Putting a third cap on the rifle and keeping it down with

F. C. SELOUS :
* " Travel and Adventure in South-East Africa " : 1893 : p. 430.
† " African Nature Notes and Reminiscences " : 1908 : p. 138.
‡ ibid. p. 142.

his thumb, he again galloped in pursuit. In a couple of minutes he had overtaken one of the bulls in a patch of short, thick, mopani bush in which the beast halted, wheeled round, and on catching sight of the horse immediately made for it with nose outstretched and horns laid back. Turning his horse broadside on, Selous endeavoured to obtain a shot just between the neck and the shoulder which would have either knocked the buffalo down or made him swerve, but his horse instead of standing commenced to walk forward, though taking no apparent notice of the buffalo. His own description of what followed in the next few seconds is as follows: * " in another instant his outstretched nose was within six feet of me, so, lowering the gun from my shoulder, I pulled it off right in his face, at the same time digging the spurs deep into my horse's side. But it was too late, for even as he sprang forward the old bull caught him full in the flank, pitching him, with me on his back, into the air like a dog. The recoil of the heavily-charged elephant-gun with which I was unluckily shooting, twisted it clean out of my hands, so that we all, horse, gun, and man, fell in different directions .... The buffalo, on tossing the horse, had stopped dead, and now stood with his head lowered within a few feet of me. I had fallen in

* " A Hunter's Wanderings."

a sitting position, and facing my unpleasant looking adversary. I could see no wound on him, so must have missed, though I can scarcely understand how, as he was so very close when I fired".

" However I had not much time for speculation, for the old brute, after glaring at me a few seconds with his sinister-looking bloodshot eyes, finally made up his mind and, with a grunt, rushed at me. I threw my body out flat along the ground to one side, and just avoided the upward thrust of his horn, receiving, however, a severe blow on the left shoulder with the round part of it, nearly dislocating my right arm with the force with which my elbow was driven against the ground, and receiving also a kick on the instep from one of his feet. Luckily for me, he did not turn again, as he most certainly would have done had he been wounded, but galloped clean away". This was a wonderfully lucky escape for Selous, but his horse was so badly injured that he was obliged to shoot it.

Count Samuel Teleki shot 79 buffaloes between the 24th April, 1887, and 27th May, 1888, on his expedition in Eastern Equatorial Africa which resulted in the discovery of Lakes Rudolf and Stefanie.* Count Teleki had a large caravan to feed which necessitated a great deal of shooting.

* " Discovery of Lakes Rudolf and Stefanie " · 1894 Vol. II : Appendix I.

CHAPTER IV

ASIATIC BUFFALOES

THE Indian buffalo like the Indian elephant has for centuries been domesticated, and except for the fact that the tame animals are slightly smaller they have remained identical with their wild brethren.

In a wild state they are without doubt dangerous animals to pursue. In his book, " The Highlands of Central India ", Captain J. Forsyth says: " As is the case with most wild beasts, it all depends, I believe, on whether you press them hard or not . . . . If followed up on foot, I believe the buffalo to be a much more dangerous opponent than the bison ". Sir Samuel W. Baker, whose experience of them in Ceylon is probably unrivalled, says: " There is a degree of uncertainty in their character, which much increases the danger of the pursuit. A buffalo may retreat at first sight with every symptom of cowardice, and thus induce a too eager pursuit, when he will suddenly become the assailant ".

The methods of hunting the Asiatic buffalo are naturally governed by the nature of the country.

BIG GAME SHOOTING RECORDS

In India they may be shot from elephants in such districts as the high grass jungles of the Terai and Assam, whilst in more open country they are usually killed by stalking. In the Sunderbuns, when the country is flooded, they have on occasions been shot from boats. They are at all times water loving beasts and in the neighbourhood of the lakes, swamps and extensive plains of Ceylon they seem to have formerly existed in greater numbers than in any other part.

It would appear that the record bag of Asiatic buffaloes was made in Ceylon by Sir Samuel W. Baker, who shot about 200 of these animals during the eight years he spent in that country.

In writing about the life of Sir Samuel Baker in Chapter II, I have already pointed out that no game diaries of his exist, so that we do not know the exact figures of all the game he shot. During a part of his residence in Ceylon he did keep game books, but the authority for the bag of buffaloes quoted occurs on page 61 of his book "The Rifle and Hound in Ceylon". The greater part, if not the whole of that book, was written while Baker was still in Ceylon, so that it is quite probable that he actually shot a good many more than 200.

There seems to be no record of any other man devoting himself to buffalo shooting in the way that Baker did. The fact that they were to be found in their greatest numbers in the hottest and usually most unhealthy parts of the country never deterred him. On the wide plains, devoid of the slightest cover, which stretched for miles along the edge of Lake Minneria, he delighted in attacking the herds or single old bulls on foot, and armed usually with two powerful but single-barrelled muzzle-loaders.

One of his earliest experiences with these beasts was productive of an incident that must surely be unique in the history of big game hunting. His own description of that afternoon and evening's sport is I think one of the clearest and finest descriptions of a sporting incident that has ever been written, but it is too long to quote in full.

On this occasion Baker and his brother, armed only with a couple of shot guns for which they carried a few balls, were tempted to attack a herd of buffaloes in the open. Between them they disabled one bull, and while his brother was disposing of this animal Baker gave chase to another. At the end of about a mile he brought the animal to bay in some shallow water at about fifteen paces distance. At this time his knowledge of these animals was slight and he says he would willingly have betted ten to one on the shot. His last two balls were fired however with no further effect than to cause the bull to advance a few more paces towards him. Facing the beast with his empty gun he instinctively felt for his hunting knife but realized its uselessness. Not daring to move, and keeping his eyes fixed on his antagonist, he gave a loud whistle as a signal to his brother. The next few minutes he describes as follows: the buffalo " seemed aware of my helplessness, and he was the picture of rage and fury, pawing the water, and stamping violently with his fore-feet.

" This was very pleasant! I gave myself up for lost, but putting as fierce an expression into my features as I could possibly assume, I stared hopelessly at my maddened antagonist.

"Suddenly a bright thought flashed through my mind. Without taking my eyes off the animal before me, I put a double charge of powder down the right-hand barrel, and tearing off a piece of my shirt, I took all the money from my pouch, three shillings in sixpenny pieces, and two anna pieces, which I luckily had with me in this small coin for paying coolies. Quickly making them into a rouleau with the piece of rag, I rammed them down the barrel, and they were hardly well home before the bull again sprang forward. So quick was it that I had no time to replace the

ramrod, and I threw it into the water, bringing
my gun on full cock in the same instant. However, he again halted, being now within about
seven paces from me, and we again gazed fixedly
at each other, but with altered feelings on my
part. I had faced him hopelessly with an empty
gun for more than a quarter of an hour, which
seemed like a century. I now had a charge in
my gun, which I knew if reserved till he was
within a foot of the muzzle would certainly floor
him . . . . . At this moment I heard a splashing
in the water behind me, accompanied by the hard
breathing of something evidently distressed. The
next moment I heard B's. voice. He could
hardly speak for want of breath, having run the
whole way to my rescue, but I could understand
that he had only one barrel loaded and no bullets
left. I dared not turn my face from the buffalo,
but I cautioned B. to reserve his fire till the bull
should be close into me, and then to aim at the
head.

"The words were hardly uttered, when, with the
concentrated rage of the last twenty minutes, he
rushed straight at me. It was the work of an
instant. B. fired without effect. The horns were
lowered, their points were on either side of me,
and the muzzle of the gun barely touched his
forehead when I pulled the trigger, and three

---

shillings' worth of small change rattled into his hard head. Down he went, and rolled over with the suddenly checked momentum of his charge. Away went B. and I as fast as our heels could carry us, through the water and over the plain, knowing that he was not dead but only stunned "

Baker subsequently had some great days with these animals. One day in June, 1847, he killed 10 buffaloes and finished up the day by shooting 5 teal and some snipe on his way home.*

His favourite weapon for this sport was his powerful two-grooved single rifle by Gibbs which weighed 21 lbs. and fired a 3 oz. spherical or 4 oz. conical bullet propelled by 16 drams of powder. He brought off some wonderful shots with this rifle. On one occasion he came across two large bulls fighting and as the two beasts ranged side by side he took a shot at the shoulder of the nearest. Both were killed by the one shot, the ball lodging in the tough hide of the second animal, having passed clean through the bodies of both. On another occasion, with a view to testing its power and accuracy at long ranges, he tried a shot at a buffalo walking through the shallows of Lake Minneria, as the splash of the ball in the lake would enable him to see the margin of error. The result of this shot he

* "The Rifle and Hound in Ceylon": 1864: p. 154.

describes as follows: "We watched the smooth surface of the water as the invisible messenger whistled over the lake. Certainly three seconds elapsed before we saw the slightest effect. At the expiration of that time the buffalo fell suddenly in a sitting position, and there he remained fixed; many seconds after, a dull sound returned to our ears; it was the 'futt' of the ball, which had positively struck him at this immense range. What the distance was I cannot say; it may have been 600 yards, or 800, or more. It was shallow water the whole way; we, therefore, mounted our horses and rode up to him. Upon reaching him, I gave him a settling ball in the head, and we examined him. The heavy ball had passed completely through his hips, crushing both joints, and, of course, rendering him powerless at once.

"The shore appeared full half a mile from us on our return, and I could hardly credit my own eyes, the distance was so immense, and yet the ball had passed clean through the animal's body.

"It was of course a chance shot, and even with this acknowledgment, it must appear rather like the 'marvellous' to a stranger; that is my misfortune, not my fault. I certainly never made such a shot before, or since; it was a sheer lucky hit, say at 600 yards; and the wonderful power of the rifle was thus displayed in the ball perforating the large body of the buffalo at this range. This shot was made with a round ball, not a cone ".

I have dealt with Sir Samuel W. Baker's experiences with the Asiatic buffaloes at some length as I can find no record of any other man devoting himself to their pursuit as a separate sport in the way that he did.

The largest bag of buffaloes made in a single day in India that I can find recorded was made one day in April, 1895, by the Maharajah of Cooch Behar and his party which consisted of the following: Baron Massow, Messrs. Seton-Karr, Hawkins, Firman, Lehmann, Apcar, Perree, P. Sen, E. Ezra and A. Ezra. Beating with a line of elephants and shooting of course from howdahs the day's bag amounted to 8 buffaloes and 1 tiger.*

Another notable day's sport was obtained in 1899 when 7 buffaloes were accounted for in a bag of 15 head of big game. I quote the Maharajah of Cooch Behar's own description of this great day: † " the 7th March ushered in the grandest day's shooting I have ever had. This was at Dhowbeel, where, soon after mid-day, we

* The Maharajah of Cooch Behar " Thirty-seven Years of Big Game Shooting in Cooch Behar, The Duars, and Assam " : 1908 : page 154.

† ibid pp 236-7-8

had thirteen head of big game accounted for, a record which I really think has never been beaten. Here are the details: one bull bison, two bull rhino. and three cows, two bull buffalo and five cows. Two Barasingh stag were also shot. Excepting the Barasingh, all these beasts were turned out of one patch of grass. We had great luck in getting the bull bison. He was seen by the howdah elephants before we had actually caught them up, and he turned out to be the same that had bested us some years back. He was a rare old bull and stood 18 hands 1 inch at the shoulder". In this year the Maharajah's shooting party included: H.R.H. The Count of Turin, Prince Teano, Count Carpenetto, Lord Lonsdale, Lord Elphinstone, Sir Henry Tichborne. Messrs. Hall Watson, Vanderbyl, Gurdon, Plowden, Prall and Rajey.

In 1886, in a month's shoot during February and March, the bag of bigger game consisted of 28 buffaloes, 19 rhinos, 9 tigers, 5 bears, and 1 bison,* and between the years 1871 and 1907, 438 buffaloes were shot on the Maharajah's domains.†

* The Maharajah of Cooch Behar. "Thirty-seven Years of Big Game Shooting in Cooch Behar, The Duars, and Assam" : 1908 : p. 40.
† ibid. p 449.

CHAPTER V

AFRICAN RHINOCEROSES

FOR the purposes of this book it is convenient to deal with the white or square-mouthed, and the black or prehensile-lipped rhinoceroses in one chapter, as so many of the early writers on African sport refer to these animals without particularizing as to the species, and many believed that there were two distinct varieties of the black rhinoceros. The idea of there being two species of the latter animal was probably a native view; animals in which the posterior horn was equal or nearly equal in length to the anterior being regarded by them as a separate race.

With regard to the question of danger attaching to the hunting of these beasts, Mr. F. C. Selous in " African Nature Notes and Reminiscences " has written as follows : " That a certain proportion of the vanished race of South African rhinoceroses of the prehensile-lipped species were of a morose and savage temper, and therefore dangerous animals to encounter, I will not for one moment attempt to deny, for there is a great deal of evidence that this was the case. But what I do think is that many writers have taken the character of the exceptionally vicious animals they met with as typical of that of the whole species ". Referring to the race throughout the whole of its range, he says: " Everywhere it seems to have been and to be a stupid, blundering, bad-sighted, but keen-scented beast; in the great majority of cases doing its best to avoid human beings, but always liable to become savage when wounded, like elephants, lions, and buffaloes, and sometimes being really bad-tempered and savage by nature, and ready to charge unprovoked at the sight or scent of any one approaching it ". Few men can have had a greater experience of these animals than A. H. Neumann, and in an interesting contribution to the " Great and Small Game of Africa " he gives his opinion as follows: " As regards the much-disputed question, to what degree the rhinoceros is a dangerous beast, the result of my experience and observations is very decidedly to convince me that, under ordinary circumstances and with proper caution, there is not much risk in shooting him, and that the danger is not to be compared in any way with that attending the pursuit of the elephant. At the same time, there is always a possibility that one may charge, and there is therefore a certain amount of excitement in the sport; and instances are not rare of men having been badly injured by these beasts ".

With regard to the white rhinoceros, Capt. Cornwallis Harris considered the species to be nearly as dangerous as the black and he says that he found it "subject to the same paroxysms of reckless and unprovoked fury" and "often fully as troublesome as its sable relative". The majority of observers, however, have regarded it as the reverse of vicious, and Mr. W. D. M. Bell who found them very plentiful on the west bank of the Nile describes them to me as "quite inoffensive" and "unlike the pugnacious black".

I think it is probable that C. J. Andersson shot more rhinoceroses than any other man, though just how many he did kill we do not know, and it is doubtful if he knew the exact number himself. He has stated however that he killed "many scores". His writings show that he shot nearly 60 of these animals in a few months, and during one night at Tunobis in the space of five hours he shot 8 (independently of other game).*

CHARLES JOHN ANDERSSON

Andersson was a Swede by birth but half English by parentage, and in his early days

* " Lake Ngami."

undertook several hunting expeditions in his native land. He went to South Africa in June, 1850, and the rest of his life was practically devoted to hunting and exploration in that country, where he eventually died. The books he wrote are well known, and in the course of his career he must have shot an enormous quantity of game. Much of his shooting was done at desert fountains and waterholes at night, and it it not surprising therefore that he shot large numbers of rhinos as these animals are water-loving, water-drinking beasts, and in times of drought are attracted from large tracts of country to such scattered drinking places as there may be. There is no doubt that this was a most deadly method of shooting in South Africa and Andersson practised it extensively. In addition to his huge bag of rhinoceroses, mentioned earlier in the chapter, he describes one night when he bagged no less than 3 hartebeests, 2 pallahs, and 5 zebras in the course of a few hours, and he says, that had he felt inclined, he could have shot double the number.*

Andersson regarded the black rhino as a decidedly dangerous beast. He describes animals of this species as not only of " a very sullen and morose disposition " but also " subject to sudden

* " Lake Ngami " : p. 237.

79

paroxysms of unprovoked fury, rushing and charging with inconceivable fierceness, animals, stones, bushes—in short any object that comes in their way ". In spite of the great numbers he shot, however, he only experienced one serious adventure with these animals. On this particular occasion he was injured and nearly lost his life through too closely approaching and throwing a stone at an animal that he had previously wounded.

He shot a fair number of elephants and most of his hunting of these animals was done on foot, but in this branch of sport I do not think he met with anything like the same success as some of his contemporaries. Often poorly equipped, he at times suffered from intense hardship and privation, but he was at all times a careful observer and his writings must always be regarded as affording a true picture of the South African fauna of his time.

WILLIAM COTTON OSWELL

Among the early English hunters in South Africa was W. C. Oswell, who on two occasions narrowly escaped with his life from encounters with rhinoceroses. He was certainly one of the most successful hunters of his time and he had a very wide experience of both species of rhino.

AFRICAN RHINOCEROSES

In one season he and Major Frank Vardon shot 89 of these animals.*

Born in 1818 he entered the service of the East India Company in 1837 and whilst in India enjoyed such sports as coursing the Indian fox with Afghan greyhounds, pig sticking and snipe shooting. He also obtained his first experience of big game hunting, shooting sambur, axis, bear, etc.

In 1844, when reduced from 12 st. 2 lb. to 7 st. 12 lb. by many attacks of Indian fever, caught during a shooting expedition in the valley of the Bhavany River, he was sent to the Cape as a last chance by the Madras doctors. The splendid climate of South Africa rapidly restored his health and the ensuing eight years were the most adventurous of his life. With the exception of a period in 1847 and 1848 which was spent in India and England, he devoted himself to hunting and exploring in South Africa. He was the first white man to penetrate many portions of the country, and in 1849, in company with Livingstone and Murray of Lintrose, he crossed the Kalahari and discovered Lake Ngami.

So reticent was Oswell in communicating his knowledge and experience to the world, that it was only under the pressure of his great friend Sir Samuel W. Baker and others that he was

* H. A. Bryden : " Gun and Camera in Southern Africa " : p. 490.

F

eventually persuaded to write his South African reminiscences for the Big Game volumes of the Badminton Library. He died before the publication of this work and Baker wrote a biographical sketch from which the following extracts are taken: " His character, which combined extreme gentleness with utter recklessness of danger in the moment of emergency, added to his complete unselfishness, ensured him friends in every society; but it attracted the native mind to a degree of adoration . . . . . I have always regarded Oswell as the perfection of a Nimrod. Six feet in height, sinewy and muscular, but nevertheless light in weight, he was not only powerful, but enduring. A handsome face, with an eagle glance, but full of kindliness and fearlessness, bespoke the natural manliness of character which attracted him to the wild adventures of his early life.

" He was a first-rate horseman, and all his shooting was from the saddle, or by dismounting for the shot after he had run his game to bay ".

Whilst he was in South Africa, Oswell had some hundred and eight horses and the weapon with which he did practically the whole of his shooting was a muzzle-loading 10-bore by Purdey. This gun was double-barrelled, weighed 10 lbs. and burnt five or six drachms of fine powder. In after years he lent it to Sir Samuel Baker, who described its appearance as follows: " This grand old gun exhibited in an unmistakable degree the style of hunting which distinguished its determined owner. The hard walnut stock was completely eaten away for an inch of surface; the loss of wood suggested that rats had gnawed it, as there were minute traces of apparent teeth. This appearance might perhaps have been produced by an exceedingly coarse rasp. The fore-portions of the stock into which the ram-rod was inserted was so completely worn through by the same destructive action, that the brass end of the rod was exposed to view. The whole of this wear and tear was the result of friction with ' wait-a-bit ' thorns!

" Oswell invariably carried his gun across the pommel of his saddle when following an animal at speed. In this manner at a gallop he was obliged to face the low scrubby ' wait-a-bits ', and dash through these unsparing thorns, regardless of punishment and consequences, if he were to keep the game in view, which was absolutely essential if the animal were to be ridden down by superior pace and endurance. The walnut stock thus brought into hasty contact with sharp thorns became a gauge, through the continual friction, which afforded a most interesting proof of the untiring perseverance of the owner, and of the immense distances that he must have traversed at the highest speed during the five years' unremitting pursuit of game upon the virgin hunting-grounds of Southern Africa ".

Oswell always strove to obtain the closest quarters with all game and to this he owed his great success, but in the case of dangerous animals the personal risk was greatly increased as the margin for escape was very limited. On one occasion he had his horse killed under him by a buffalo and on another a lioness landed on his horse's quarters, but as the horse dashed away an overhanging branch swept both Oswell and the lioness to the ground. His unusual experience with and narrow escape from a white rhinoceros he describes thus : " Returning to camp one evening with a number of Kafirs, tired and hungry after a long day's spooring elephants, which we never overtook, I saw a long-horned mahoho standing close to the path. The length of his horn, and the hunger of my men, induced me to get off and fire at him. The shot was rather too high, and he ran off. I was in the saddle in a moment, and, passing the wounded beast, pulled up ten yards on one side of the line of his retreat, firing the second barrel as he went by from my horse, when, instead of continuing his course, he stopped short, and, pausing an instant, began to walk deliberately towards me. This movement was so utterly unlooked for, as the white rhinoceros nearly always makes off, that, until he was within five yards, I sat quite still, expecting him to fall, thinking he was in his ' flurry '. My horse seemed as much surprised at the behaviour of the old mahoo as I was myself, and did not immediately answer the rein, and the moment's hesitation cost him his life and me the very best horse I ever had or knew; for when I got his head round, a thick bush was against his chest; and before I could free him, the rhinoceros, still at the walk, drove his horn in under his flank, and fairly threw both him and his rider into the air ". Quickly snatching a spare gun from an after-rider Oswell finished the rhino, but his horse was so badly injured that he had to shoot it. He himself was but little hurt, but in an adventure with a black rhinoceros the consequences were more serious. This incident he describes as follows: " The rhinoceroses were now within twenty yards of me, but head on, and in that position they are not to be killed except at very close quarters, for the horns completely guard the brain, which is small and lies very low in the head . . . . . I had so frequently seen their ugly noses, when within eight or ten yards of the gun, turn, tempted by a twig or tuft of grass to the right or left, and the wished-for broadside thus given, that I did not think anything was amiss until I saw that if the nearer of those now in front of me, an old cow, should forge her own length once more ahead, her foot would be on me. She was so near that I might possibly have dropped her with a ball up the nostril, and, had she been alone, I should probably have tried it; but the rhinoceros, when he charges, nearly always makes straight for the smoke of the gun, even though the hunter is concealed, and I knew that if No. 1 fell, No. 2, who was within four or five yards of her, would in all probability, be over me before the smoke cleared. In the hope that my sudden appearance from the ground under her feet would startle her and give me a chance of escape, I sprang up; the old lady was taken aback for a moment and threw up her head with a snort. I dashed alongside of her to get in her rear; my hand was on her as I passed; but the shock to her nerves was not strong enough, for before I had made ten yards she was round, and in full chase.

" I should have done better to fire into her as I went by, but it had not occured to me, and it was now too late; in my anxiety to escape, to put it as mildly as may be, I had neglected my best chance, and paid the penalty. I was a fast runner; the ground was in my favour, but in thirty yards from the start she was at my heels. A quick turn to the left saved me for the moment, and, perhaps, by giving my pursuer my flank instead of my back, my life too. The race was over in the next; as the horned snout came lapping round my thigh I rested the gun on the long head and, still running, fired both barrels; but with the smoke I was sailing through the air and remember nothing more, for I fell upon my head and was stunned ".

Two gashes, one eight inches long and right down to the bone, kept Oswell to his bed for nearly four weeks.

There is nothing in his own writings or in the two volumes of his life written by his eldest son, W. Edward Oswell and published in 1900, to indicate the full extent of his bag, but it is certain that he must have killed a great quantity of game. The fact that he and Murray fed six hundred starving natives of the Ba-kaa for seven weeks, and then sent them back to their kraals with an abundant supply for future use, gives some idea of what he must have shot. On one of his day's hunting for these people he shot 2 elephants, 1 rhinoceros, and jointly with Murray 14 hippopotami, whilst one of his drivers shot a giraffe and a quagga.

BIG GAME SHOOTING RECORDS

Writing of the white rhinoceros, he says: "I have seen these long-horned square-nosed creatures in herds of six and eight, and when in need of a large supply of meat for a tribe, have shot six within a quarter of a mile, with single balls".

It is interesting to note that every head of game he killed in Africa, save three elephants, was eaten by man. He had some good days with elephants and he records shooting 4 bulls in a day with at least 500 lbs. of ivory, and the heaviest pair of tusks he got weighed between 230 and 240 lbs. the pair.

The conclusion of his expedition in 1852 was the termination of his career as a hunter. In 1860 he married and thereafter lived a retired life at his home at Groombridge where he died in 1893.

The number of rhinoceroses of both the black and the white species that formerly existed in South Africa must have been immense. Anderson mentions 9 white rhinos having been killed in a single day by a European near Walfish Bay, and in "The Recollections of William Finaughty" there is mention of a day in which Finaughty and Gifford, failing early in the day to find fresh elephant spoor, turned their attention to other game and between them made a bag of 13 rhinoceroses, 1 lion, and 1 lioness. In the north-west of the

AFRICAN RHINOCEROSES

Transvaal white rhinos were very plentiful and Capt. Cornwallis Harris mentions that on one occasion in 1836 when travelling through the Magaliesberg district no less than 80 were seen during a day's march, while on his way from the Limpopo to a hill half a mile distant 22 were counted, of which 4 were killed in self-defence.

The practical extermination of both the black and white rhinoceros in all the countries between the Limpopo and the Zambesi took place between the years 1872 and 1890, owing largely to their horns suddenly attaining a considerable commercial value. About 1880, traders in Matabeleland began to employ native hunters to shoot them, and as an indication of the extent of this trade, F. C. Selous has written as follows : " One trader alone told me that he had supplied four hundred Matabele hunters with guns and ammunition and between 1880 and 1884 his large store always contained great piles of rhinoceros horns —of all sorts and sizes, often the spoils of over a hundred of these animals at one time, although they were constantly being sold to other traders and carried south to Kimberley on their way to Europe ".

At the present time the sole survivors of the southern white rhinoceros are I believe about 26 specimens preserved in the Umfolsi Reserve in

Northern Zululand. Whether this particular reserve will continue to be maintained seems somewhat doubtful, but is to be hoped that the future of these few beasts will in some way be safeguarded.

Mr. W. D. M. Bell, whose career as an elephant hunter I have dealt with in the first chapter, has kindly supplied me with the following notes on his experiences with rhinoceroses in Equatorial Africa: " Regarding my bag of black rhino I find that out of a total of 63 killed no less than 41 were shot when presenting some sort of menace to either myself or to a line of porters or to an encampment. Of the remainder only three were killed for food, thus indicating the richness of the other and better meat harvest, while the remainder were chiefly killed for making sandals or for rewarding natives with shield pieces. In my time the horn was not worth taking unless of unusual size.

" During my elephant hunts west of the Nile on the banks of that river the white rhino was very plentiful. The greatest number I ever saw in one day was eleven but I saw some every day. They were quite inoffensive, unlike the pugnacious black, and hardly ever required shooting. Other meat was plentiful and I killed three only ".

The rhinoceros is not usually regarded as one

AFRICAN RHINOCEROSES

of the great prizes of big game hunting, but Major Frank Vardon who accompanied W. C. Oswell on some of his travels in South Africa seems to have taken the keenest pleasure in their pursuit. Oswell says of him: " Vardon was the most enthusiastic rhinoceros hunter; he filled his wagon with horns as I did mine with ivory; he used to shoot four or five every day, and there was always a freshness about the sport to him which seemed remarkable. He was an all-round shot, but best at rhinoceros ".

Vardon does not appear to have ever written about his travels and sport so that little is now known concerning him.

According to Count Samuel Teleki's game book he shot 80 rhinoceroses in Eastern Equatorial Africa between 24th April, 1887, and 27th May, 1888.*

Count Teleki, a nobleman with a large estate in Transylvania, was a well-known sportsman and in 1887-88 he undertook the important journey of exploration which culminated in his discovery of the Lakes Rudolf and Stefanie.

* " Discovery of Lakes Rudolf and Stefanie ": 1894: Vol. II: Appendix I.

CHAPTER VI

LIONS

THE lion is certainly one of the most dangerous animals to be found in Africa, and in the opinion of F. C. Selous it is the most dangerous of all. This great authority considered that when once a lion is stopped it never refuses battle, whereas, in his experience, buffaloes and elephants try to get away unless very severely wounded. Selous' experience of lions was chiefly gained in South Africa, but there seems no reason to suppose that their character varies to any great extent in any part of Africa. He has pointed out that though more casualties resulted from hunting buffaloes, quite fifty of the latter animals were killed in South Africa to every one lion.

Other hunters of experience have regarded the buffalo or the elephant as being more dangerous, but the casualties resulting from lion hunting in East Africa have certainly been very numerous, though doubtless many occurred to men who were novices. Mr. W. D. M. Bell states that he was told " that in one year out of about forty visiting sportsmen who devoted themselves seriously to lion hunting, twenty were mauled. Of these twenty, more than half were killed or died from the effects of wounds ". This great hunter goes on to say: " The lions of that period were extraordinarily bold and courageous. In the early morning on those huge plains I have walked steadily towards a troop of lions numbering a score. Just as steadily walked away the troop—no hurry or fear of man ".*

Whatever opinions may be held regarding the dangers of lion hunting, it is certain that the greatest desideratum in their pursuit is the ability to shoot both quickly and straight.

Before giving details of the largest bags of lions it is necessary to say something concerning the various methods of hunting that have prevailed in different parts of the Continent.

In the early days in South Africa most hunting parties were accompanied by a few powerful mongrels, and the services of these were generally called upon in any attack on lions, the dogs assisting in tracking and bringing the animals to bay; though few men in that part of the country seem to have hunted lions as a separate sport. The most successful men of those days were mostly shooting for a living, and lions therefore were not often shot unless they became a menace

* " The Wanderings of an Elephant Hunter " : 1923 : p. 176.

BIG GAME SHOOTING RECORDS

to an encampment or were met with casually.
It would not appear that they were ever so
plentiful in South Africa as in East Africa where
all the largest bags have been made.   In such
strongholds as the vast reed-beds of the Athi in
the latter country they were at first hunted on
foot, but the difficulties were so great that ponies
and dogs came to be used. " Riding them " is
doubtless one of the finest forms of hunting and
Sir Alfred Pease has said of this sport: " I loved
galloping and rounding them up for others to kill
as much as I enjoyed anything in my whole life ".
Packs of dogs have also been used in East Africa
in bringing the lions to bay, which greatly reduces
the danger to the human element.

In Somaliland they are mostly tracked on foot,
and in every part of the country they can of
course be shot at " a kill " from bomas.

So far as I have been able to ascertain, the largest individual bag of lions made in one day was
obtained in 1921 by H.H. the Maharajah of Datia,
in Laikipia. Mr. Jim Fey of Naivasha was the
hunter employed by the Maharajah, and no less
than 18 lions were killed by the latter in one night,
shooting from a boma of thorn over a zebra
carcass.   The total for that night was 34 lions and
2 leopards, killed by four guns.*

* Hamilton Snowball · *in litt*. 8th May 1931.

94

LIONS

Another very large bag obtained by similar means occurred on the Kinangop above Naivasha early in 1922, when a troop of lions killed four donkeys belonging to Mr. Jim Fey. With his partner he sat up in a boma adjacent to the dead donkeys and together they shot 14 lions in an hour and a half.*

An unexpected, though notable, bag was made some time prior to 1910 by two young Dutchmen who were travelling in a trek wagon towards Nakuru. They were besieged by a troop of lions on the open plain and, without stopping the wagon, one brother drove the oxen with a rifle by him, whilst the other lay in the tail of the wagon and shot 8 lions and 4 lionesses.*

On Sir Alfred Pease's farm on the Kapiti Plains a party once killed 14 lions in a single day (1911-12).† Sir Alfred informed Mr. J. G. Millais that he himself had only killed 14 lions and joined in 11 "partnerships". Having killed all the specimens he wanted he preferred to give his friends every opportunity of enjoying good sport. Sir Alfred is of course a big game hunter of great experience. A first-rate horseman and a first-rate shot, he has killed between eighty and a hundred varieties of big game.

* Hamilton Snowball : in litt 8th May 1931.
† J. G. Millais : " The Life of F. C Selous " · 1913 · p 191

BIG GAME SHOOTING RECORDS

In South Africa the largest bag for a single day that I have found recorded was made by that famous elephant hunter William Finaughty. On the day in question he tracked and shot 7 lions, and this feat was performed with a muzzle-loader.*

On the 20th January, 1909, the Danish hunter, Karl Larsen, shot 7 lions in the space of two minutes in Portuguese South-west Africa. He was on the track of a wounded bull elephant in the Quillenques district of Benguella when he came upon fresh lion spoor and immediately afterwards he encountered the animals themselves. Armed with a double-barrelled .600 rifle by W. J. Jeffery & Co. he accounted for the 7 lions with nine cartridges.†

Who the first man to kill a hundred lions may have been I do not know, but Amen-Hotep III is said to have killed 102 fierce lions in the first ten years of his reign (1400-1390 B.C.).‡ In connection with this subject of bags of lions, Mr. J. G. Millais obtained much interesting information which he set forth in his book, " The Life of F. C. Selous ", and he gave details concerning the methods employed by the hunter who has

* " The Recollections of William Finaughty."
† " O Benguella " : 6th March 1909.
‡ H. S. Gladstone : " Record Bags and Shooting Records " : 1922 : p. 6 (quoted from " Ancient Records of Egypt : The Historical Documents " : Vol. II : 1906 : No. 865).

probably killed a greater number of lions than any other man. I refer to Paul Rainey, who claims to have killed over two hundred lions. Mr. Millais says: "Paul Rainey's methods of hunting lions with a large pack of hounds can hardly come into the true category of lion-hunting where risks are taken. The dogs, it is true, were often killed or wounded; but as a friend who had taken part in these hunts remarked: ' It was just like rat-hunting, and about as dangerous '. It is true that one man, George Swartz (formerly a German waiter at the Norfolk Hotel, Nairobi), was killed in one of these hunts, but the accident was singular. Swartz was a very bold fellow and moved close in in thick bush when the dogs had a lion at bay one day in the Kedong in 1912. The lion ' broke bay ', and either intentionally charged Swartz or ran over to him by chance as he worked the cinema-camera. The beast gave the man one bite in the stomach and then left him, but the unfortunate fellow died shortly afterwards of his wounds ".*

It is difficult to obtain exact statistics concerning bags of lions and, indeed, this remark applies to all kinds of game. Some men do not keep records of their sport, others are reticent in discussing what they accomplished, and " partner-

* J. G. Millais : " The Life of F. C. Selous " : 1918 : p. 192.

ships " or animals accounted for by the combined efforts of a party all add to the difficulties of ascertaining exact figures.   It is probable that the man who has killed the greatest number of lions by ordinary methods of hunting* is Mr. Clifford Hill, a resident farmer in East Africa, who also acted as professional hunter to many "safaris". His brother, Harold D. Hill, informed Mr. Millais in March, 1918, that Clifford Hill had been in at the death of 160 lions though he constantly allowed some friend to have first shot.   Harold D. Hill, who for several years managed Sir Alfred Pease's farm in East Africa in addition to his own, stated that he himself had been in at the death of 135 lions, but as in the case of his brother's total this does not represent the number of animals on which he had drawn first blood.† Doubtless both brothers could have increased their personal totals had they been so minded.

According to F. C. Selous, that famous Boer hunter Petrus Jacobs killed well over one hundred lions during the course of his life in South Africa.   Unlike many of the Boer hunters, Jacobs was always ready to attack lions and when over seventy-three years of age he was badly mauled by one.   This animal seized him by the thigh and threw him to the ground biting

* See also p. 103
† J. G. Millais "The Life of F. C. Selous" 1918 · p. 191

him fearfully. He was also bitten in the left arm and hand but all the time his three powerful dogs "were worrying the lion's hind-quarters, and soon made it so rough for him that he left his human foe to attack them ". Within two months of this incident " the sturdy old fellow was again able to ride on horseback ".* Petrus Jacobs was one of the most experienced elephant hunters in South Africa and some further notes concerning him will accordingly be found in the first chapter.

Mr. W. D. M. Bell has recorded the doings of an old Sikh ex-soldier and his son at the time the Uganda Railway was being constructed.† " It was when the Government had offered a large reward for every lion killed within a mile on either side of the railway. Fired with the prospect of immediate wealth, this old man obtained a Rigby-Mauser .275, and he and his son took to hunting lions. There were then in East Africa troops of lions sometimes over twenty strong. Knowing from the permanent-way gangs of coolies the likeliest spots, the hunters began their operations. These consisted of building shelters from which to fire by night, and they were generally situated close to reed beds known to be used by lions. At first the shelters were quite

---

* F. C. Selous · " A Hunter's Wanderings in Africa "
† " The Wanderings of an Elephant Hunter " 1923 · pp 175/6

BIG GAME SHOOTING RECORDS

elaborate affairs affording considerable protection. Familiarity taught them that no protection was necessary, and latterly the cache was merely a ring of boulders over which one could fire from the prone position. The old man could imitate a goat or a cow to perfection, but whether it was desire on the part of the lions to eat goat or cow, or merely curiosity to find out what the strange noise was, must remain a mystery. Certain it is, though, that the Sikhs' cache was a sure draw. The young fellow shot straight and true, and lion after lion succumbed. In nine months these two men claimed the reward on some ninety skins. On about forty-five the reward was actually paid, there being some doubt as to whether the remainder were killed within the mile limit ".*

Hunting in Somaliland and British East Africa, Lord Delamere is believed to have killed between fifty and sixty lions.† Towards the close of last century this fearless and skilful hunter made his historical journey across Somaliland and into British East Africa, where he became one of the pioneer settlers and founders of Kenya Colony.

Mr. William Judd, one of the greatest professional hunters of East Africa, is said to have killed 48 lions in South and East Africa‡ and to

* According to the brochure published by Messrs. Chas. A. Heyer & Co. of Nairobi, Mr. J. A. Hunter has shot 84 lions.
† J. G. Millais : " The Life of F. C. Selous " : 1918 : p. 192 (quoted from a letter from Sir Alfred Pease).
‡ ibid. p. 190.

have been in at the death of 43 others.   A
magnificent shot, Judd only experienced one
narrow shave in the making of this bag.   This
incident occurred in the Gwas N'yiro bush when
he was hunting with F. C. Selous in 1909.   The
history of this encounter was subsequently given
by Judd to J. G. Millais, who has described it as
follows: " It appears that Selous and Judd were
out together one day and disturbed two lionesses,
which disappeared in thick forest.   Selous at once
galloped after them and outdistanced Judd, who
came somewhat slowly cantering behind, as he
did not wish to interfere with Selous.   All at
once, from the side of the path, Judd saw a great
yellow body come high in the air from the side of
the game-trail.   He had no time even to raise his
rifle from the position across the saddle-pommel,
but just cocked it up across and pulled the trigger.
One of the lionesses, for such it was, had
apparently crouched and allowed Selous to pass,
and had then hurled herself upon the second
hunter.   By a fine piece of judgment, or a happy
fluke, Judd's bullet went through the lioness's
eye and landed her dead at his feet.   His horse
swerved.   He fell off, and found himself standing
beside the dead body of his adversary ".

A. B. Percival, the well-known game warden,
and author of two excellent books on big game,

is said to have shot 50 lions during his residence in East Africa, and in one season in Somaliland, Colonel Curtis killed 27.*

In 1892-3 Colonel Arthur Paget and Lord Wolverton made a trip in Somaliland of five months' duration. Subsequently, Lord Wolverton wrote an account of this expedition which was published in 1894 under the title of "Five Months' Sport in Somaliland". A careful perusal of this work shows that these two sportsmen accounted for 32 lions during this period.

Major J. Stevenson Hamilton killed by himself between 50 and 60 lions, 47 of which he walked up alone on foot in South Africa. "In the three months of August, September and October, 1920, he walked up and shot 16 lions in the Transvaal".† Concerning Major Hamilton, Sir Alfred Pease has written as follows: "Major Hamilton has had many experiences in the Sudan and elsewhere, and there are few better authorities on African zoology". Sir Alfred then says: "Yet Hamilton would say that there is another man living named Fraser, whom I knew in my Transvaal days, whose knowledge is probably superior to that of any man past or present. Fraser is now growing old, but is a man of

* J. G. Millais : "The Life of F. C. Selous" : 1918 : p. 190.
† Sir Alfred E. Pease : "Edmund Loder—A Memoir" : 1923 : p. 28.

remarkable physique and with abnormal powers of observation; he has spent twenty years in South Africa and twenty-five previously in India; he can write excellent descriptive letters, sketches and paints beautifully, and has a most intimate acquaintance with the life histories and habits of South African fauna, yet he never has and never will make use of his knowledge and talents for the benefit of the outside world. The secrets he has discovered and the knowledge acquired in his long life of diligent and intelligent observation in the wilds will die with him ". I have quoted the foregoing at some length as it goes to show how some men of vast experience leave little or no record of their achievements behind them, and one can never be absolutely certain that statistics which appear to constitute a record have not at some time been exceeded.

As this book was on the point of going to press I received a letter dated 17.12.31 from Col. Stevenson-Hamilton, who states that though he does not know the exact number of lions that he has killed during the thirty years he has now spent in Africa, he believes it to be about 200. Owing to pressure of space I am unable to quote his letter in full, but the following extracts are of particular interest. All these lions were killed hunting alone and on foot, that is accompanied by never more than two trackers. Of these, perhaps twenty have been shot at night by sitting up over their own kills or at water holes. For the last twenty years he has used an ordinary long barrelled .303 service rifle and with this he has killed about 130 lions. His largest bag at one go was five, and his best, four black-maned lions.

That great African hunter, Mr. W. D. M. Bell, was mainly concerned with elephants, but in some interesting notes that he has kindly furnished me with, he says: " With regard to lions I merely killed any that caused annoyance, such as roaring round camp, stampeding porters, and so forth. The total so killed is 25 ".* Leopards he shot. when he came across them, provided he was not close to elephants at the time, or by waiting for them at water-holes, etc. Mr. Bell shot 16 leopards during the course of his hunting career. I have already indicated in the chapters devoted to African elephants and African buffaloes that Mr. Bell is a rifle shot of outstanding ability, it is therefore particularly interesting to know his views on lion hunting. I quote the following from his most excellent book, "The Wanderings of an Elephant Hunter", in which he says: " The reason of the high

* W D. M. Bell : *In litt*. 23rd March 1931.

mortality among those who hunt lions casually is, I think, the simple one of not holding straight enough. Buck-fever or excitement, coupled with anxiety lest the animal should slip away, is probably the cause of much of the erratic shooting done at lions. This frequently results in flesh wounds or stomach wounds, which very often cause the lion to make a determined charge; and there are a great many things easier to hit than a charging lion. Great care should be taken to plant the bullet right. The calibre does not matter, I am convinced, provided the bullet is in the right place. Speaking personally, I have killed sixteen lions with .256 and .275 solid bullets, and, as far as I can recollect, none of them required a second shot ".

F. C. Selous shot 31 lions himself* and joined in the killing of 11 others, but though his bag of these animals is of no very great magnitude he made a close study of their natural history, and his writings on the subject remain unchallenged as the most detailed and authoritative works that we have.

* See also Chapter VIII.

CHAPTER VII

TIGERS

" THERE is a romance and a devilishness about a tiger possessed by no other Indian animal," so says Major-General A. E. Wardrop, and doubtless ninety-nine men out of every hundred, who have shot big game in India, will agree with him.

Tigers, according to their different habits, may be divided into three classes: those which habitually live on game alone; those which prey upon cattle; and the considerably smaller proportion that kill and devour human beings. The last-named are usually old animals of either sex which have difficulty in procuring their normal food owing to some disability, and there is no reason to suppose that they prefer human flesh.

Tigers may be hunted with a line of elephants, the rifles either shooting from howdahs or from positions towards which the animals are driven, or they may be driven by beaters on foot, though the latter proceeding is only possible where the jungle will admit of the men maintaining line.

TIGERS

They are also shot by sitting up over a " kill "
or " bait " or by watching for their arrival at
pools where they are known to drink.   In some
parts where the cover is so continuous as to make
driving impracticable, tigers are surrounded with
nets and shot from outside or inside.   Tiger
shooting on foot is a most dangerous form of sport
and though not usually systematically followed,
it is sometimes resorted to.

Though the range of the tiger includes the
Caucasus, Northern Persia, the Malay Peninsula,
Sumatra, Java, Manchuria, Korea, etc., they are
by no means plentiful in most of these countries
and all the largest bags have been made within
the Indian Empire.

The most productive tiger shoot appears to
have occurred on the occasion of His Majesty
the King's visit to Nepal in 1911.   I take the
following details of the wonderful sport enjoyed
from Major-General Nigel Woodyatt's delightful
book, " My Sporting Memories ": " King George
arrived in the Nepalese Tarai on the 18th December, and killed two tigers on that date.   With the
exception of Sunday the 24th, His Majesty shot
every day, leaving for Calcutta on the evening of
the 28th December.   The total bag of King
George and his suite was, tiger, 39; rhino, 18;
bear, 4; barking deer, 1 ".   On 20th December,

in the Chitawan Valley, the day's bag amounted to, tiger, 7; bear, 2; rhinoceros, 2. " Of the tiger, King George got five, and Sir Colin Keppel and Captain Godfrey Faussett one each. The two rhino were killed by the King and the Duke of Teck. The couple of bear by Sir Horace Smith-Dorrien and Captain Godfrey Faussett ".

So far as I know, this day's bag of 7 tigers has only once been exceeded and that was in 1897 in the same country. I quote "The Field" of the 5th June, 1897, for the details of the shoot in question : " The shoot organised for Sir Baker Russell in Nepal during the last week of April by the kind permission of Sir Bir Sham Sher, Prime Minister of Nepal, appears to have been quite a phenomenal one in those parts. Unfortunately Sir Baker was himself unavoidably prevented from attending it, but the remainder of his party, which consisted of Colonel Garbott, C.O. of the 2nd Bengal Lancers; Major Ellis, R.E.; Major Bewicke-Copley (Sir Baker's military secretary); Major Smith-Dorrien, Derbyshire Regiment; and Capt. Browne Clayton, 5th Lancers, were lucky enough to secure twenty-three tigers, four cubs, and four leopards in fourteen days, besides a large quantity of various kinds of deer and birds ". Referring to this same fortnight's sport

TIGERS

General Woodyatt says:[*] "It was in this shoot that the guns in the beat arrived at the 'stops' with eight full grown tiger killed".

Another bag of 7 tigers as the result of a single day's shooting was made by the Maharajah of Cooch Behar's party in February, 1907. The following is the Maharajah's own description of the day's sport: [†] " The big shoot commenced on the 18th at Saralbhanga River. Our party consisted of Their Excellencies the Earl and Countess of Minto, Lady Eileen Elliot, Adam, Dunlop Smith, Crooke-Lawless, Bulkeley, Mackenzie, Graham, Rajey, Hammond, Lyall, Perrée, Sujey and myself ".

" The first day was a glorious one. Before lunch we had three tigers padded and bagged another four in the afternoon, making in all seven tigers."

On the 16th March, 1903, the Maharajah and his party, which at that time included Lord and Lady Lonsdale, had another great day. Shooting the Reserves on the Jorai nullah, 5 tigers were bagged within twelve minutes,[‡] and on two separate occasions in 1902 the day's bag included 4 tigers.

* " My Sporting Memories ". 1923 : p. 20
† " Thirty-seven Years of Big Game Shooting in Cooch Behar, The Duars, and Assam " : 1908 : pp. 411-414.
‡ Ibid. p. 354.

BIG GAME SHOOTING RECORDS

Between 1871 and 1907, 365 tigers were killed on the domains of the Maharajah of Cooch Behar, and it is interesting to note that during the same period the total number of leopards killed amounted to 311.*

A notable bag to one rifle was made by Mr. R. P. Cobbold in the Central Provinces in 1897. Between March 1st and June 1st, Mr. Cobbold shot 11 tigers, 3 panthers, 4 buffaloes, 2 bison, 4 bears, 2 sambhur and cheetah, making a total of 26 head of big game. The tigers were all obtained by driving and it is noteworthy that no animal wounded escaped. Mr. Cobbold was shooting with a .577 by Holland and Holland.†

It is impossible to say definitely who has killed the greatest number of tigers. Of that great hunter, Sir Henry Ramsay, General Woodyatt says: " I do not think he knew how many tiger he had shot. Probably several hundreds and he never sat up for a tiger, if he could help it ".‡ Mangal Khan, an Indian gentleman in the United Provinces, informed Sir John Hewett in 1921 or 1922 that he had seen over 900 tigers killed. Concerning Mangal Khan, General Woodyatt writes: § " His ancestral home (he is a big land-

* " Thirty-seven Years of Big Game Shooting in Cooch Behar, The Duars, and Assam " 1908 p 449
† " The Field " 1st July 1897
‡ " My Sporting Memories " 1921 p 16
§ ibid pp 23/24

110

holder) is in Pilibhit in the U.P. and the name he gave it is Sherpur (tiger town). A grand sportsman he is too. He has been known to clap his hands in order to turn a tiger to some other stop ".

Lieut.-Colonel A. E. Ward, a mighty hunter with a vast knowledge of Indian game, and several of the Indian Princes must also have shot enormous numbers of tigers, but certainly one of the most noted tiger-hunters of modern times was Colonel Faunthorpe. Exactly how many tigers he killed does not appear to be known, but it is believed to be over 300.

LT.-COL. JOHN CHAMPION FAUNTHORPE

Col. Faunthorpe will always be remembered as one of the greatest figures in the annals of Indian sport. He excelled as a hog-hunter and as an all-round horseman and judge of horse-flesh, whilst as a big game hunter and rifle shot, and particularly as a howdah shot, it is doubtful if he ever had a superior in India.

Educated at Rossall he gained a reputation as a marksman before leaving school and later he shot for Oxford. Subsequently he joined the Indian Civil Service and arrived in India in 1892. In 1894 he was posted to Banda where he had his first experience of big game hunting. In 1896 he was in Cawnpore and here he was introduced to pig-sticking, which sport he pursued with zest, whenever opportunity offered, until the outbreak of the " Great War ". He was in the final of the Kadir Cup in 1899 and during the course of his career he also speared leopards, swamp deer, cheetah, hog deer, etc.

Faunthorpe was a successful exhibitor at the horse shows in Upper India and he was also a Steward of the Lucknow Race Course. In 1912 he won the Civil Service Cup with his pony "Devon" which he had imported from Australia on his own judgment.

In 1901 he was given charge of the district of Bahraich in Oudh where he enjoyed excellent shooting in the vast forests bordering on Nepal, and later he was posted to the Naini Tal district, which area included some of the finest tiger country in Northern India, and whilst there he organized many big shoots for distinguished visitors.

On being transferred to Muzaffarnagar in 1905, Faunthorpe found himself in a district, the ravines of which harboured a great number of panthers. With the assistance of the local Banjaras, who were first-rate men at tracking the panthers, he was most successful with these animals. Whenever a panther had been located word was sent to Faunthorpe, who immediately galloped to the spot; the Banjaras's dogs were then put into the panther's lair with a view to making it bolt, thus giving Faunthorpe the chance of a shot. This was carried out with such success that in a little over a year he is believed to have shot nearly a hundred panthers.*

In 1907 he was appointed to Kheri and he subsequently enjoyed such big game shooting as falls to the lot of very few men in India. The exact number of tigers that Faunthorpe killed does not appear to be definitely known, but it is stated in that excellent biographical sketch which appeared in " The Hoghunter's Annual " that " the number that he shot must be over three hundred ".†

Faunthorpe's skill with the rifle was of a quite exceptional order. To be able to stand on the seat of a howdah and wait for the rush of a stag through a thinner patch of jungle, where a fleeting glance of its head might be obtained, and then to kill it with a shot through the neck at some 200 yds., is an accomplishment that few men would attempt with the slightest hope of success, but Faunthorpe has been known to do it.

* " The Hoghunters' Annual " : Vol. IV : 1931 : p. 30.
† Ibid. Vol. IV : 1931 : p. 30.

BIG GAME SHOOTING RECORDS

Not only was he brilliant as a lightning-shot at moving targets, but, if circumstances demanded, he was equally capable of infinite patience in firing, even with his game in full view. The following instance quoted from General Wardrop's classic "Modern Pigsticking" well illustrates his capacity in this respect. Faunthorpe was beating for a well-known tigress whose mate had been killed by General Wardrop and a brother officer some years before "She dodged the line for hours, but, getting bored, climbed on to a stack of grass bundles to see how the hunt went. Faunthorpe aimed at her for about two minutes while his elephant swayed; at last he got a bead he was satisfied with, and knocked her over, stone dead, at a distance of over 200 yards".

At Bisley in 1929 he shot for the Indian Eight in the Kolhapore Cup and he won the Running Deer competition against all comers.

Before the War, Faunthorpe commanded the United Provinces Horse and at the outbreak of hostilities in 1914 he was on leave in England. Of his various services in connection with the War it is unnecessary to speak, but he was awarded the C.B.E. and the Military Cross, and in 1922 he received the exceptional distinction and honour of being appointed A.D.C. to H.M. the King.

TIGERS

On his return to India he became Commissioner at Lucknow and much of his spare time was then spent in conjunction with Arthur S. Vernay collecting specimens for the Natural History Museums of Chicago and New York. For the furtherance of this object he was placed on special duty, and in 1922-23 the Vernay-Faunthorpe Expedition was carried out. With the assistance of the Government of India, the Ruling Princes, and Local Governments, this expedition was a great success and a representative collection of the big game animals of India, Burma and Nepal was obtained.

In connection with this work Col. Faunthorpe shot some lions in the Gir country in Kathiawar and he is one of the very few men who have ever done so. Mr G. M. Dyott, F R G.S., who accompanied the expedition as photographer, obtained some excellent cinematograph pictures for use in the Museum Lecture Hall. These pictures were exhibited to the public for a short period and Mr. Dyott spoke concurrently with the presentation of the film. Colonel Faunthorpe retired from the service in 1925, but in connection with the work of collecting specimens he returned to India in 1929 when he contracted pneumonia and died on the 1st December of that year.

In 1930, Mr. Vernay generously gave the

BIG GAME SHOOTING RECORDS

National Rifle Association sufficient capital to provide a Colonel Faunthorpe Memorial Cup, and it would be difficult to conceive a more fitting memorial to this remarkable man.

Sir Edmund Loder, in the course of a letter written in 1875, refers to Colonel Baigrè, who, he says, has killed 195 tigers;* but I can find no other references to this individual.

H.H. the Maharajah of Bikaner is said to have shot 143 tigers up to the year 1930,† and other men, though probably not very many, have killed over a hundred.

Many capable and experienced sportsmen have assisted in the killing of great numbers of tigers, though they may have accounted for no very great number themselves. Thus, Major-General Woodyatt writes:‡ " Few men now living have seen as many tiger shot as Sir John Hewett . . . . the number is very close on to two hundred and fifty, and in localities so wide apart as Assam, Central Provinces, Nepal and the United Provinces ", but being a most unselfish sportsman, he himself had only killed about forty. Of Sir John Campbell, who has seen nearly 200 tigers killed, of which he has shot at least 60, he

* Sir Alfred E. Pease : " Edmund Loder—A Memoir " : 1923 : p. 176.
† " Sunday Express " : 5th October 1930.
‡ " My Sporting Memories " : 1923.

116

goes on to say: " He once got three tigers in three shots in rather over three minutes. Two were shot in the neck and one in the forehead, and none of the three required a second shot ".

Sir Bindon Blood is said to have been at the death of over 150 tigers, of which 52 have fallen to his own rifle.*

Tigers are so rarely met with by chance and shot when after other game that I am tempted to recall an experience that befell that well-known surveyor and explorer of unknown country, Colonel H. G. C. Swayne, then a young lieutenant, in the jungles of West Mysore in 1889. I do not put it forward as a record, though it is particularly interesting as it relates to the first tigers that he shot.

On the day in question he was after sambar stag in high tree jungle with bushy undergrowth, when he suddenly smelt something dead, and thinking it might be a kill of some sort he decided to investigate it. Almost immediately a tigress passed him diagonally from his right, obviously going towards the " kill ", or whatever it was. When the beast was about sixty yards to his right front, he fired, hitting her through the ribs. She was down wind, and never saw him,

* Major-General Nigel Woodyatt : " My Sporting Memories " : 1923 : p. 19.

but on being hit, she raced away for sixty yards across his front, and then all was silence. He then sent his shikari up a tree to get a view, while he remained below with rifle ready, but the native saw the tigress lying dead.

They then proceeded to skin the animal together, but suddenly the shikari stole quietly away, his idea being to go and investigate the cause of the smell.

Swayne went on with the job of skinning till at length the native returned, excitedly pointing. He had discovered a dead sambar, and a male tiger was moving about near the meat.

Quickly circling down wind to a tree, from behind which the native had spied the tiger, Swayne steadied his rifle against the upright trunk and waited. Thirty yards away the tiger rolled about playfully by the kill, but no more than fleeting glances of the tail, or a leg, were obtainable, so the Indian picked up a small stone and threw it, but without result. The beast must have been heavily gorged not to have heeded the shot at the tigress, or else it must have come quickly from a distance while they were quietly skinning the tigress.

As the small stone thrown by the native had produced no result, Swayne picked up a piece of rock weighing about six pounds and heaved it at the tiger, striking the animal on the ribs. The tiger roared and stood looking to Swayne's left. At that moment he fired, hitting him in the ribs, at which the beast raised himself to his full height, gnawing his own shoulder; then he galloped away through the grass straight down wind, springing high, like a dog does, to look about him over the grass.

Again the shikari ascended a tree, when he quickly spotted the tiger lying dead.

The tiger, the tigress, and the tree from which Swayne had fired formed an equilateral triangle the sides of which measured no more than about 30 yards.

In furnishing me with the details of this incident, that officer has been good enough to give me some other particulars. I quote his notes in full as they are not only of great interest, but his remarks concerning the statistics of big game shooting in general coincide so closely with the views which prompted the writing of this book, and which I have endeavoured to express in the introductory chapter. Under date of 26th July, 1931, he says: "So far as my records go, they cover 44 years in two phases; from 1884 to 1897, years of exploration surveys in Africa for the Government, when there were often thirty or forty men to provide with meat for a year or more at a time; from 1898 to 1927—about 40 smaller private trips in Asia and Africa in order to complete collections, see new countries, and meet new tribes. Beginning with the subject of the big predatory cats—tigers, lions, and leopards—one met them by chance when on foot and alone or when accompanied by two or three natives, who did the main part of the tracking. Camp arrangements were inexpensive, consisting of a low explorer's tent without furniture, or bivouacking on the ground in the open. The occasions of meeting the great cats are rare; and the modest number of seventeen was accounted for in over forty years, though one saw many more than one got. Time and finances were limited, and although one saw a great deal of the effects of their depredations on natives, and was constantly coming on their spoor, one sometimes refrained from attacking them when a head scarcely showing in the grass made shooting too difficult. On one of the rare occasions when I happened to have another white man with me, I was knocked over and mauled by a lioness and saved very gallantly by my brother. Our two surveying parties had met, and we had heard of lions at a tribal meeting and gone out together.

" In Somaliland I had conclusive though melancholy proof of what a pair of lions can do when really after human beings, as in one month a pair killed eight people: the first a young bride clawed out of a hut at night; and the last my head camelman torn from a mule when galloping in broad daylight alone through the glades of the Ogaden bush. Both of these I helped to bury, and tribal evidence disclosed six other human beings having been killed in the interval between these two cases. In that Ogaden journey of many hundred miles one seemed to be always having to treat wounds inflicted on the inhabitants by lions.

"I never joined big shoots or drives, for reasons of economy, and only once shot a tiger from a tree, at night, in Rajpipla, through the kind help of the Assistant Resident at Baroda.

"It is not uncommon for District Officials in India, as a public duty in the course of their career, to kill a hundred or more tigers by organized drives, young buffaloes being tied up at likely spots for bait; on the principle of sacrificing one for all; and tigers so localized are driven out by a line of elephants and shot from the howdah; it is very exciting sport, but beyond the means of most soldiers.

"Personally, I should be content to see all the predatory cats poisoned, for the sake of the natives and stock.

BIG GAME SHOOTING RECORDS

" Going on to discuss game, not naturally predatory, but occasionally destructive to human life or property, which includes elephant, rhinoceros, and various sorts of bears, some two dozen of this class were accounted for; and as for other animals, when looking for a special trophy, as most men hailing from India do, one has on some trips travelled thousands of miles by land or sea, coming back with but a single trophy worthy of the name."

Colonel Swayne then goes on to say: " Your investigation into the statistics of sport is especially interesting just now, when ' big game shooting ', on the strict principles prevailing in the past, is already a dying pursuit; the reasons being easy access, by air or road, to game haunts by undesirable people; the broadcasting of firearms among natives who shoot everything they see; and settlers on the land destroying game which is inimical to crops, on economic grounds. Another reason is that there is a growing objection to all cruel sports; and travel films have made wild animals of distant countries no longer a novelty.

" That the extermination of game cannot be laid at the door of genuine ' big game hunters ' can be proved by a simple calculation—A man who in a lifetime bags a score of the big cats and

TIGERS

say about 200 of other game is really not reducing the game; for a tiger, lion, or leopard will average four kills a month at least; he lives say four years at his prime; so that twenty big cats would have killed 3,840 head of game or cattle and the ' big game hunter ' comes out of it with a credit balance of some 3,640 saved, if not created by himself, let alone their posterity.

" The best chance of really seeing these wild animals in future will be in Government sanctuaries in selected climates of the world, where, with the improved travel facilities, people will in the future be able to visit them without being shocked by the sight of tropical animals lame with rheumatism, or arctic animals shut up in stuffy dens in summer."

I think these notes by Colonel Swayne make an interesting supplement to his own excellent books, " Seventeen Trips through Somaliland and a visit to Abyssinia " and " Through the Highlands of Siberia ", and to his other writings. He can look back a long way. He carried out the first explorations of what afterwards became British Somaliland as long ago as 1884-87, and later was a member of the inaugural expedition of the Imperial Chartered Company which took over Mombasa and Lamu villages from the Arabs in 1888, at the time when Stanley and

123

Emin Pasha reached the East Coast from Wadelai; and 1915-17 found him re-employed on active service in France and Flanders with an R.E. Labour Battalion, when he was mentioned in despatches and awarded a C.M.G. I do not know when he first began exploring with theodolite and rifle, but as recently as 1927 he and Mr. Louis Defries, who is well known in South Africa, unexpectedly encountered elephants after dark when returning to a ranch from shooting and narrowly escaped being trampled on. I think his career stands for all that is best in big game hunting and is in accordance with the highest traditions of that army of fine soldier-sportsmen whose education in the arts of the chase commenced with service in India.

CHAPTER VIII

OTHER AFRICAN GAME ANIMALS

PROBABLY the greatest slaughter of game ever
accomplished in any part of the world, as the
result of a single hunt, took place in South Africa
on the plains of the Orange Free State. I quote
Mr. H. A. Bryden for a brief description of the
event: * " In 1860 when the Duke of Edinburgh
(then Prince Alfred) was taken to the eastern part
of the Orange Free State, a great hunt was got
up in his honour.   One thousand of Moroka's
Barolong, then dwelling at Thaba Unchu, drove
in the game from a large tract of country.   It
was computed that at least 25,000 head of game
were in sight of the sportsmen; black and blue
wildebeest, Burchell's zebras, quaggas, ostriches,
blesboks, hartebeests and springboks were to be
seen all charging hither and thither in affrighted
squadrons, and raising clouds of dust.   The
number of game slain that day ran into thousands
—6,000 some people say; several natives were
trampled or crushed to death by a charging herd

* " Gun and Camera in Southern Africa ": 1893.

125

of zebras; while others sustained broken limbs ". This great drive must certainly have afforded a wonderful though barbaric spectacle, but with this one allusion to native hunts we can pass on to what has been accomplished by white hunters.

It would obviously be impossible to ascertain the record bag for each and all of the game animals of Africa, and, even were it possible, the figures would be of very little interest in the great majority of cases, but that is not the purpose of this chapter. Its object is to give some details concerning two hunters whose great all-round experience of African hunting merits special reference and whose careers have not been dealt with in earlier chapters.

It is generally agreed that the hunter who amassed the finest collection of African trophies ever shot by one man was F. C. Selous, and it is therefore appropriate to deal with him first.

F. C. SELOUS

The name of this great sportsman, naturalist, and explorer is probably more widely known than that of any other hunter of his generation. Other men have killed more elephants, lions, and other dangerous game, and others have been better shots, but as an accurate and skilled observer of nature, capable of imparting his knowledge to others, Selous had outstanding ability. His writings and lectures attracted a large public, and his highly trained powers of observation and deduction were so strictly accurate that everything that he wrote came to be regarded as authoritative, and therefore of the utmost value. All his books are written in a direct and straightforward manner, yet they impart vivid pictures of the scenes and incidents described, and they must always rank as classics in their particular line.

The history of Selous's life is so well known, firstly through the agency of his own books, and secondly through the excellent biography written by J. G. Millais ("The Life of Frederick Courtenay Selous, D.S.O." 1918), that I do not propose to deal more than very briefly with the main features of his career, but the concluding lists concerning the game that he shot may prove of interest.

Born in 1851 and educated at Rugby, Selous spent a couple of years on the Continent before going out to South Africa, and it was at Untersberg in Bavaria, in October, 1870, that he shot his first big game, two chamois falling to his rifle. At the age of nineteen he landed in South Africa, determined to become an elephant hunter, which at that date meant hunting on foot, since the majority of the elephants had retreated into the

" fly " country of the interior.   Armed with an
old muzzle-loading, smooth-bore, single barrel
elephant gun, weighing about 16 lbs., and firing
a 4 oz. spherical ball, and endowed with a
magnificent constitution and great fleetness of
foot, Selous soon made his mark as a hunter; but
elephants were rapidly becoming scarce, and as a
paying proposition their pursuit was not what it
once had been.   Save for one holiday in England
in 1875 Selous continued hunting and trading
with a fair measure of success until 1881, when he
returned home and shortly afterwards published
the first of his books, " A Hunter's Wanderings
in Africa ".   By the end of 1881 he was back at
the Cape however, and the next six years were
mainly devoted to procuring specimens for
museums and for his own and other private
collections.   It was during this period that he
obtained many of the finest specimens in his unrivalled collection of South African game, and
most of his hunting during these years was done
on horseback.   In 1890 he led the pioneer expedition of the Chartered Company into Mashonaland,
and the two following years were taken up by
survey and similar work.   In 1892 he returned
home and in 1893 he published " Travel and
Adventure in South-East Africa ", which covered
that period of his life which followed the publica-

tion of his first book. The same year saw him back again in Rhodesia and he assisted in the suppression of the first Matabele insurrection. He then decided to come home for good and shortly afterwards he married, but in 1895 he returned to Rhodesia to take up the management of an estate, and, as it happened, to serve through the second Matabele War.

In 1894-95, and again in 1897, Selous visited Asia Minor, and his subsequent expeditions in pursuit of big game in various parts of the world may be summarised as follows: 1897 and 1898 Wyoming, 1899 Transylvania, 1900 Canada and Newfoundland, 1901 Newfoundland, 1902 Sardinia, 1902-3 Kenya Colony, 1904 the Yukon, 1905 Newfoundland, 1906 the Yukon, 1907 Asia Minor and Norway, 1909 Kenya Colony, 1911 Bahr-el-Ghazal, Sudan, and 1911-12 Kenya Colony.

At the age of sixty-four, Selous went to East Africa to take his part in the Great War. He quickly distinguished himself, being promoted to a captaincy in the Royal Fusiliers and subsequently being awarded the D.S.O. for his achievements in the field.

In January, 1917, he was shot dead while leading his company through the bush against an enemy four times their strength. Thus died a great Englishman for the country that he loved, in a country that he can hardly have loved less.

Of his many services to the Empire and to science, of his almost miraculous escapes both from wild beasts and unfriendly natives, and of his brave, chivalrous, and modest character there is no need to speak, since all these aspects of his noble and adventurous life have been dealt with by others.   Nothing could have been more significant however of the admiration and esteem in which he was held than the presentation to the Natural History Museum by the subscribers of the memorial to him, which took the form of a bust in bronze and which was unveiled on the 10th June, 1920.   During his lifetime he had given many valuable specimens to the museum, and in 1919 his own vast collection was presented to the nation by Mrs. Selous.   With hardly any exceptions the 443 specimens of African game and the 81 specimens from Europe, Asia, and North America were shot by Selous himself.

I have not found it possible to give the exact figures of all the game that he killed, but in the lists that follow I have given what I believe to be accurate details for some of the larger African game animals, together with a list of all the African species that he shot, whilst the American, European, and Asiatic lists represent, I think, the full extent of his bag in those countries.

OTHER AFRICAN GAME ANIMALS

I have carefully compiled these lists from the following sources of information: his own books; " The Life of F. C. Selous " by J. G. Millais, 1918; the " Catalogue of the Selous Collection of Big Game in the British Museum (Natural History) " by J. G. Dollman, B.A., 1921; and from the article " Captain Selous and his Trophies ", Country Life, January 13th, 1917.

List of certain of the larger game animals of Africa shot by F. C. Selous

Elephants . . .	106
Buffaloes . . .	177
Lions	31
White Rhinoceroses . .	23
Black Rhinoceroses . .	28
Giraffes	67

Antelopes

Eland	120
Kudu	60
Sable	125
Roan	88
Gemsbuck . . .	65
Tsessebe . . .	139

NOTE.—In connection with these statistics it should be remembered that Selous started his career as a professional hunter and for many years he and his followers practically depended on what he shot, whilst the elephants were of of course killed for their tusks.

BIG GAME SHOOTING RECORDS

.

List of the various species of African game shot by F. C. Selous

Elephant
White Rhinoceros
Black Rhinoceros
Hippopotamus
South African Buffalo
East African Buffalo
Lion
Leopard
East African Serval
South African Cheetah
South African Giraffe
Uganda Giraffe
Reticulated Giraffe
Mashonaland Eland
East African Eland
Sudan Derby Eland
Kudu
Lesser Kudu
Sable Antelope
Roan Antelope
Gemsbuck
Ibean Beisa
Coke Hartebeest
Nakuru Hartebeest
Jackson Lelwel Hartebeest
Selborne Rooi Hartebeest
Lichtenstein Hartebeest
Bontebok
Blesbok
Tsesebe, or Sassaby
Tiang
Jimela
Wildebeest, or Gnu
Blue Wildebeest
White-bearded Gnu
Natal Duiker
Ravine Red Duiker
Blue Duiker
Common Duiker
Abyssinian Duiker
Klipspringer

Oribi
Powell-Cotton's Oribi
Nile Oribi
Cape Steinbuck
Transvaal Steinbuck
East African Steinbuck
Grysbok
Kenya Pigmy Antelope
Desert Pigmy Antelope
Zululand Pigmy Antelope
Cavendish's Dik-Dik
Lesser Jubaland Dik-Dik
Nyika Dik-Dik
Smith's Dik-Dik
Vaal Rhebok
Reedbuck
Ward's Reedbuck
Rooi Rhebok
Chanler's Reedbuck
Waterbuck
Defassa
Lechwe
Uganda Kob
White-eared Kob
Puku
Pala, or Impala
Jubaland Impala
Thomson's Gazelle
Black-snouted Thomson's Gazelle
Grant Gazelle
Springbuck
Gerenuk
Highland Bushbuck
Chobe Bushbuck
Cape Bushbuck
Nyala, or Ingala
Zambesi Situtunga
Zebra
Grevy's Zebra
Wart-Hog

OTHER AFRICAN GAME ANIMALS

List of big game shot by F. C. Selous in North America *

Moose	6
Wapiti	9
Osborn's Caribou . .	7
Newfoundland Caribou .	9
White-tailed Deer . .	2
Mule Deer . . .	7
Prongbuck . . .	2
Canadian Lynx . .	1
Alaskan Timber Wolf .	2

List of big game shot by F. C. Selous in Europe

Red Deer . . .	6
Reindeer . . .	5
Chamois	8
Sardinian Mouflon . .	5

List of big game shot by F. C. Selous in Asia Minor

Eastern Red Deer, or Maral	1
Wild Goat, or Pasang . .	6

W. C. BALDWIN

One of the few early hunters in South Africa to leave us actual details of their bag was William Charles Baldwin and he has only given the

* Excluding a few animals shot for meat.

statistics of his last expedition in 1860, but as an indication of the sport that South Africa afforded at that date it is of particular interest.

Baldwin, who was a good shot and a first-rate horseman, went to Africa with the principal object of elephant hunting, but though he was fairly successful in this respect he never penetrated into Matabeleland which was then the main stronghold of elephants in South Africa. Concerning his early life, he has said: " The love of sport, dogs, and horses was innate in me. From the age of six I had my two days a week on a pony with the neighbouring harriers ". Following his schooldays he spent some years on farms in Scotland, but he did not settle seriously to the life and eventually he decided to go to Natal where he landed in December, 1851. From this date till 1860 he hunted from Zululand to the Zambesi and west to Lake Ngami.

Like most South African hunters of his time Baldwin did a good deal of night shooting at water-holes and desert fountains, and his best night's sport occurred during his last trip in 1860. On this particular night he shot 3 buffaloes, 1 white rhinoceros bull, 1 quagga, 1 lion, and 1 elephant.*

* .W. C. Baldwin : " African Hunting and Adventure from Natal to the Zambesi " : 1894 : p. 390.

OTHER AFRICAN GAME ANIMALS

On this same expedition one of his native hunters, Boccas, killed 3 harrisbuck (sable antelopes) with one bullet. This extraordinary feat was performed at night, shooting by moonlight.

The following is a list of game killed by himself and three native hunters on his last expedition in 1860.*

61	Elephant
2	Hippopotamus
11	Rhinoceros, white
12	Rhinoceros, black
11	Giraffe
21	Eland
30	Buffalo
12	Harrisbuck (Sable Antelopes)
14	Roan Antelope
2	Gemsbuck
9	Koodoo
4	Waterbuck
1	Hartebeest
12	Tsessebe
18	Impala
1	Blesbuck
25	Springbuck
12	Blue Wildebeest
2	Black Wildebeest

* W. C. Baldwin : " African Hunting and Adventure from Natal to the Zambesi " : 1894 : p. 422.

BIG GAME SHOOTING RECORDS

71 Quagga
 3 Duiker
10 Steinbuck
 1 Gryse Steinbuck
 1 Fall Rheebuck
 2 Striped Eland
 4 Lion
   Etc.

CHAPTER IX

OTHER INDIAN GAME ANIMALS

THE GREAT INDIAN RHINOCEROS

OF the three species of rhinoceros that are recognized as inhabiting various parts of Asia, the great Indian rhinoceros is by far the largest. These huge beasts may stand over 17 hands at the shoulder, and with their well-defined folds of skin, large tubercles on the hind-quarters, and relatively short single horns, they can hardly be described as handsome animals. Their range includes parts of the Nepal Terai, Cooch Behar, and Assam, and as they usually inhabit tall grass-jungles they are generally hunted for with a line of elephants. Owing to the great height of the grass the rhinoceroses form runs or tunnels which are often completely concealed from view.

So far as I have been able to ascertain the record bag of these animals was made on the 16th February, 1886, by the Maharajah of Cooch Behar and his party. The following is the Maharajah's own account of this particular day: * " A blank day on the 15th was followed

* " Thirty-seven Years of Big Game Shooting in Cooch Behar, The Duars, and Assam " : 1908 : pp. 41/42.

by a magnificent day's sport with rhino near Rossik Bheel and Chengtimari or rather half a day's, for we bagged five rhino before luncheon. I do not think this record has been beaten. Some of them showed great sport, charging through the line, and one of the new elephants got cut. The largest was 17 hds. and ½ an inch at the shoulder, 12 ft. 6 in. in length and had a girth of 112 in.". In the month's shoot which included this day the total bag of bigger game amounted to 19 rhinoceroses, 28 buffaloes, 9 tigers, 5 bears and 1 bison.*

On another occasion, on the 7th March, 1899, 5 rhinoceroses were shot. They formed part of the bag of a most remarkable day's shooting when 15 head of big game were accounted for. The following are the details† : —

    5 Rhinoceroses
    7 Buffaloes
    1 Bison
    2 Barasingh Stags
    —
Total   15 head in one day.
    —

The Maharajah of Cooch Behar : " Thirty-seven Years of Big Game Shooting in Cooch Behar, The Duars, and Assam " : 1908 : P. 40.

ibid. pp. 236-7-8.

OTHER INDIAN GAME ANIMALS

The Maharajah's party this year included the following: H.R.H. the Count of Turin, Prince Teano, Count Carpenetto, Lords Lonsdale and Elphinstone, Sir Benjamin Simpson, Sir Henry Tichborne, and Messrs. Vanderbyl, Hall Watson, Plowden, Prall, Gurdon and Rajey.

In Nepal, between the 18th and 28th December, 1911, His Majesty the King and party. bagged 18 rhinoceroses together with 44 head of other big game.*

GAUR

The Gaur, commonly called the Indian bison, is one of the grandest game animals to be found in India and the head of an old bull is a most imposing trophy. In colour the females and males are reddish brown, but as the males become adult they grow darker, and old bulls are nearly black. The hair is fine, short, and glossy, and in old bulls it becomes very thin on the back. Gaur are easily distinguished by the curved crest between the horns, which are more or less flattened, particularly in the bulls. These handsome beasts may stand 6 feet at the shoulder and their range includes all the larger forest areas of India. They prefer hilly country, and they exist in herds of about a dozen individuals, though old bulls are

* Major-General Nigel Woodyatt : " My Sporting Memories ": 1923 : p. x.

almost invariably solitary in their habits. Hunting these solitary bulls is one of the finest sports in India, and if suddenly surprised there is an element of danger in their pursuit. Gaur are shy and retiring by nature and if much persecuted they become exceedingly difficult to approach.

Owing to the nature of the ground which they inhabit they are usually hunted on foot, but in some districts they may be shot from elephants and the largest bags have been made by these means.

The record bag of bison appears to have been made by The Maharajah of Cooch Behar and his party in March, 1902, when no less than eleven of these animals were shot in a single day.

The following is his own description of this notable day's sport: * " Between thirty and forty bison had been marked down at a place north-east of Dhun Bheel .... On taking up our positions, I was the last flank stop on the east side, and as it chanced the whole herd came out in a procession past me, ending up with two bull which I killed in addition to a very fine cow. Before we had done with them, eleven bison, three bull and eight cow, were down, a record bag of bison for one day. The largest bull stood 17 hands 3¼" at the shoulder and 18 hands 3¼"

* " Thirty-seven Years of Big Game Shooting in Cooch Behar, The Duars, and Assam " : 1908 : p. 329.

at the hump, the horns were 77″ round the curve
and 18¾″ at the base. The largest cow stood
17 hands 1¼″ and had horns of 73¼″ round curves,
which, I am inclined to think, is also a record.
A Sambhur stag completed the bag ".

The Maharajah's party this year included Mr.
and Mrs. Pelham Clinton, Colonel and Mrs. Burn,
Colonel and Mrs. Baird, Mr. and Mrs. Forrest,
Lord Helmsley, Colvin, James, and Jit.

Considering that only 48 bison were killed on
the Maharajah's domains between the years 1871
and 1907 it makes this one day's sport all the
more remarkable.

BLACKBUCK

The blackbuck or Indian antelope is perhaps
the most beautiful and elegant game animal to be
found in India. They are characterized by the
spiral twist of the horns of the bucks and the dark
and handsome colour of the hair of the upper
parts in fully adult members.

They are found on the open plains where they
frequent both grass and corn-lands. Their range
extends from the foot of the Himalaya nearly to
Cape Comorin wherever the country is suitable
to their requirements. They are usually to be
seen in herds of from ten to thirty or forty with
perhaps only one fully adult buck among them.

In some districts herds of several hundred individuals are to be met with and Lydekker states that the assemblages may sometimes include thousands of individuals.

They are capable of great speed when running and the sport of coursing them with cheetahs has been fully and well described by more than one writer.

In some districts they will allow carts or even men to approach quite close and they may be shot after a concealed approach under the cover of a horse, bullock, or cart. If much harassed they soon become wild, when it is difficult to obtain other than long shots. Under all circumstances the vital points of a blackbuck afford but a small mark and accurate shooting is essential in order to kill them cleanly.

The largest bag of blackbuck that I can find recorded is mentioned by Lieut-Col. Reginald Heber Percy, though, unfortunately, he does not mention the names of those who participated in the sport. He writes as follows: * " The biggest bag of blackbuck the writer knows of was 64 bucks in 1883, by two guns in five days and a half. Of these, 10 bucks, whose horns were all over 22 in. in length, were shot by one of the sportsmen in a morning's work ".

Badminton Library : " Big Game " : 1894 : Vol. II : p. 352.

OTHER INDIAN GAME ANIMALS

Sir Edward Braddon once killed 8 blackbuck and 1 doe in a single day in Oudh.* In his excellent book, " Thirty Years of Shikar ", he refers to this day's shooting in the following terms: " I became blasé as to this form of sport after killing twenty-two bucks in three consecutive days. I might possibly have escaped from this feeling but for the result of the third day of these three; . . . . on the evening of that third day, when the carcasses of eight blackbuck and a doe (killed by a bullet that had first penetrated and killed a buck)—nine carcasses in all—were hanging from the branches of trees around my tent, I felt I was a butcher undisguised ".

SAMBAR

These massively-built deer stand from 48 to 50 inches in height, though in Ceylon, according to Sir Samuel Baker, a buck in his prime will stand fourteen hands high at the shoulder, and will weigh 600 lbs., live weight. Though most abundant in hilly districts the low country sambar are usually the largest. The body of the sambar is covered with coarse hair, dark brown in colour, and in all, the neck is more or less maned with bristly hair, which may be six inches in length.

* Sir Edward Braddon : " Thirty Years of Shikar " : 1895 : p. 270.

The antlers, which are often very rugose on the surface, are subject to considerable variation, but normally they have a single brow tine above which the beam rises nearly straight to terminate in a simple fork. They are nocturnal in their habits and are seldom found in greater numbers than two or three together, more usually being alone.

In India they are, I think, invariably killed with the rifle, but in the mountainous districts of Ceylon they may be hunted with hounds where they afford first-rate sport.

The records of sport with sambar are more difficult to ascertain than the details of the bags of the more important Indian animals, but possibly Sir Samuel W. Baker killed more of these animals than any other man.

During eight years' residence in Ceylon he kept a powerful pack of hounds at Newera Ellia and hunted sambar regularly for several years. I have already shown in some notes on his life in Chapter II that he killed approximately 400 sambar in Ceylon, and in later years he shot a good many in India, but the exact number is not known. In Ceylon he hunted entirely on foot and he never carried a spear, his hunting-knife being the only support for the dogs. This sport, as conducted by Baker, must have been

OTHER INDIAN GAME ANIMALS

most exhilarating; he described it very fully in
" The Rifle and Hound in Ceylon ", published in
1854. It was carried on at an altitude of from
6,200 to 7,000 feet in a country of plains,
separated by belts of forest, rapid rivers, water-
falls, and precipices. " Thoroughly sound in
wind and limb " says Baker, and " with no super-
fluous flesh, must be the man who would follow
the hounds in this wild country—through jungles,
rivers, plains, and deep ravines, sometimes from
sunrise to sunset without tasting food since the
previous evening, with the exception of a cup of
coffee and piece of toast before starting.   It is
trying work, but it is a noble sport; no weapon
but the hunting-knife;   no certainty as to the
character of the game that may be found; it may
be either an elk (sambar), or a boar, or a leopard;
and yet the knife and the good hounds are all that
can be trusted in ".

" It is a glorious sport certainly to a man who
thoroughly understands it; the voice of every
hound familiar to his ear, the particular kind of
game that is found is at once known to him long
before he is in view by the style of hunting. If an
elk is found, the hounds follow with a burst straight
as a line, and at a killing pace, directly up the hill,
till he at length turns and bends his headlong
course for some stronghold in a deep river to bay".

BIG GAME SHOOTING RECORDS

No doubt all lovers of dogs, and what sports-man is not, would regard sambar hunting as superior to sambar shooting, but it falls to the lot of few men to be able to maintain and regularly hunt a pack of hounds in a wild country.

CHITAL OR AXIS DEER

The chital, otherwise known as the axis, or Indian spotted deer, is probably the most beautiful member of the family to which it belongs. Their chestnut-coloured coats are spotted at all ages and seasons, and their antlers are more graceful than those of the sambar. They are to be met with both in hilly ground, and on the plains, in park-like country, and in jungle, but never far from their drinking places.

The rifle undoubtedly accounts for the greater proportion of the chital that are killed, but in suitable country they may be ridden and speared if they are caught in the early morning after a heavy feed, and they may also be coursed with grey-hounds or dogs of that type.

In the first half of the last century, these animals swarmed in certain parts of Ceylon, and it is probable that the largest bags were made at that period and in that country rather than in India.

OTHER INDIAN GAME ANIMALS

In those days Ceylon must have been a veritable paradise for the big game hunter, though owing, presumably, to some deficiency in the quality of the soil, the antler, horn, and ivory growth in the island has always been inferior compared with India. There are very few references to chital shooting as it was in those distant days, but Sir Samuel W. Baker writes as follows : * " In the vicinity of the coast, among the ' flat plains and thorny jungles,' there is always excellent shooting at particular seasons. The spotted deer abound throughout Ceylon, especially in these parts, where they are often seen in herds of a hundred together. In many places they are far too numerous, as, from want of inhabitants in these parts, there are no consumers, and these beautiful beasts would be shot to waste ".

" In the neighbourhood of Paliar, and Illepeca-déwé on the north-west coast, I have shot them till I was satiated and it ceased to be sport. We had nine fine deer hanging up in one day, and they were putrifying faster than the few inhabitants could preserve them by smoking and drying them in steaks. I could have shot them in any number, had I chosen to kill simply for the sake of murder."

* " The Rifle and Hound in Ceylon " : 1854 : p. 166.

On another occasion in this same part of the country, Baker, twice in one day, killed two deer with one shot, and in the vicinity of the Yallé river he records shooting three fine bucks and two buffaloes in a stroll with the rifle before breakfast.*

BLACK BEAR

These animals never attain such dimensions as the brown bear, and, according to Blanford, the weight of a full grown male varies from 200 to 250 lbs., though the same animal will vary greatly according to the season. They are good climbers, and, as a rule, they are vegetable feeders, though they have been known to take to killing domestic animals. They are savage by nature and prone to attack if molested, and a large number of natives are mauled annually when defending the fruit crops from invasion. They may be stalked with comparative ease or they may be driven, but they can hardly be said to afford an exciting form of sport.

No very large bags of these animals appear to have been made except by driving, but by these means Mr. P. B. Van der Byl records 40 as

* " The Rifle and Hound in Ceylon " : 1854 : p. 197.

having been shot in three days.* He writes as follows: " In November a wonderful migration of black bears takes place, from the vale of Kashmir westward into the district of Poonch; and the rajah of that place has an annual shoot lasting three or four days, at which I was once privileged to attend. A vast number of beaters are employed, and machans, or platforms, are placed in trees, so that there is little risk to the sportsman, though casualties among the beaters are not uncommon. As many as forty bears are sometimes killed in this manner in three days ".

It is probable that the biggest mixed bag of the larger game animals of India is that which I have mentioned earlier in the chapter, when, 7 buffaloes, 5 rhinoceroses, 1 bison, and 2 Barasingh stags, were shot by the Maharajah of Cooch Behar's party in a single day's sport on the 7th March, 1899.

A well mixed bag to one rifle is recorded by Lieut-Col. Reginald Heber Percy. He does not mention the sportsman's name, but in one day's shooting in 1875, the rifle in question bagged, 2 nylghai, 5 ravine deer, and 3 blackbuck; total, 10 head of game.†

Mr. R. P. Cobbold made a notable mixed bag

* " The Gun at Home and Abroad " : 1915 : Vol. IV : p. 124.
† Badminton Library : " Big Game " : 1894 : Vol. II : p. 352.

BIG GAME SHOOTING RECORDS

in the Central Provinces in 1897. Between March 1st and June 1st he accounted for the following* : —

Tigers . . .	11
Panthers . . .	3
Buffaloes . . .	4
Bison	2
Bears	4
Sambar and Chital .	2
Total . . .	26 head.

In connection with this bag it is particularly noteworthy that no animal wounded escaped.

Few records are available of the quantity of big game shot on a large area of ground over a period of years. The following statistics taken from " Thirty-seven Years of Big Game Shooting in Cooch Behar, The Duars, and Assam " may therefore prove of interest.

Total big game shot during the thirty-seven years 1871-1907.

Tiger . . .	365
Leopard . . .	311
Rhino . . .	207
Bison . . .	48

* " The Field " : 31st July 1897.

OTHER INDIAN GAME ANIMALS

Buffalo	. . .	438
Bear	. . .	133
Sambhur	. . .	259
Barasingh	. .	318

NOTE.—These figures refer to the game killed by the Maharajah of Cooch Behar and his guests.

CHAPTER X

WILD BOAR

ALTHOUGH various species of the wild pig are recognized, they form a puzzling group to zoologists, and such differences as exist, are comparatively slight. Though varying considerably in size, the chief characteristics of the wild boar are the same wherever he is found, and to the hunters of all ages he has always been regarded as game " par excellence ". The character of the boar cannot fail but to make a strong appeal to the true sporting instinct. Rarely disposed to attack unprovoked, he will, when brought to bay, charge men, dogs, horses, or elephants with a display of courage unsurpassed by any other beast. Instances of boars killing or beating off tigers are not unknown, and, once roused, only death will stay their capacity for doing mischief.

Where the nature of the ground permits of the use of horse and spear, the great sport of pig-sticking may be indulged in, but throughout a great part of the pig's range the rifle is the only practicable weapon.

WILD BOAR

Whether ridden with spear, hunted with hounds, or driven to the rifle, the boar is capable of affording sport of a high-class nature, and owing to his indomitable courage he is respected by sportsmen the world over.

The record bags of wild boar belong to the seventh century when Saxony, Bavaria, Würtemberg, and some of the smaller Duchies formed an enormous preserve for red deer, wild boar, and other game. The Elector John George I of Saxony, who reigned from 1611 to 1656, killed no less than 31,902 wild boar, whilst his son who succeeded him and reigned till 1680 accounted for 22,298.* As fuller details concerning the careers of these great hunters occur in Chapter XI, we can pass on to other records.

A notable bag of the sixteenth century was made by the Landgrave John George of Brandenburg, who in the year 1581 accounted for 501 wild boar, 677 stags, and 968 hinds.† In connection with these early records it must be remembered that the firearms of the sixteenth and seventeenth centuries were very clumsy and of an exceedingly primitive nature, though the preparations for a great boar hunt were very elaborate. Miles of movable four-foot fencing were utilized, and under the oppressive " service of the chase "

* " Sport in the Alps " : 1896 : p. 170.
† *ibid.* p. 177.

153

hundreds of peasants might be employed for weeks on end. It is difficult to conceive the amount of damage to the crops of the unfortunate peasantry which the preservation of such enormous numbers of wild boar must have caused. With no compensation for damage to property and a penalty for killing game which might well be death, the lot of the peasants must have been a hard one.

Under modern conditions of sport the record bag would seem to have been made in Poland as recently as January, 1931, and the following particulars of this shoot appeared in " The Field " of March 7th, 1931. On the estate of Prince Charles Radziwill at Maukiewicze, on January 16th, 17th and 18th, 146 wild boar and 4 wolves were killed by twelve rifles. " Of these 130 were killed in the first two days, which constitutes a record wild boar shoot. The guns were : The President of Poland (His Excellency M. Ignacy Moscicki) and three of his personal staff, Princes Charles and Jerome Radziwill, Count B. Tyszkiewiez and his son, Count Grochowlski, Count Paul Potocki, Col. Wolkowycki and Gen. Carton de Wiart ".

" The method of driving the boar is as follows : Seven hundred or so beaters form a huge perimeter, in the centre of which the rifles are aligned in a ride, some 70 or 80 yards apart. These beaters stand fast, while another lot advance into the forest and start the pig moving. The forest itself is a marsh and only passable when it is frozen over. When these beaters get to within 200 or 300 yards of the rifles they also stand fast. By that time the pig are well on the move. They then retire and advance again, and so move any that may have been left behind ". At one stand Count Paul Potocki killed twelve boar without missing, and all were shot stone dead, just behind the shoulder.

In Count Joseph Potocki's forest of Schepetowka, Volhynia, ten rifles shot over a hundred wild boar together with 77 roebucks in four days' shooting in 1912.* In this district some of the wild boar attain an enormous size, and some readers will be familiar with the magnificent mounted specimen in the Natural History Museum, London, which was presented by Count Joseph Potocki.

At the annual shoots in the Royal Forests at Gödöllo in Hungary, large bags are also made. During the drives in the winter of 1929-30, 83 boar were shot, and in the following year the bag was 73, of which eight weighed over 400 lbs., the best scaling 456 lbs.† One of the rifles on the latter

* Count, R. P. *in litt*. 15th April 1929
† " The Field " : 7th February 1931.

casion was the Maharajah of Patiala, who is probably one of the most brilliant all-round shots this time. Equally at home with the shot-gun, took part as a judge in the field trials at Ludlow in 1928 and there got 55 birds with 56 cartridges.*

In Spain one of the finest boar shoots is that of the Coto Doñana where the Duke of Tarifa concentrated the big game shooting on a single annual function. In January, 1923, during three-and-a-half days' shooting, the guns averaging twenty, accounted for a total of 101 head of big game of which 39 were wild boar.†

In Ceylon Sir Samuel W. Baker hunted these animals with his hounds and no other weapon than the hunting-knife, and so also did Snr. J. P. Falcão, a great Portuguese Nimrod. Concerning the methods and skill of the latter the Count D'Amoso has written as follows: " with his hunting-knife unsheathed ", he approaches the boar at bay " from behind, jumps upon it, grips with his knees, as in a vice, the flanks of the animal, and, while grasping with his left hand the thick mane on the creature's chine, plunges, with his right hand, the knife into the animal's body behind the right shoulder-blade, between the first

* " The Field " : 27th December 1928.
† Ibid. 1923.

156

and second ribs, killing it almost instantaneously. This he does with such courage, dexterity, and accuracy, that never has a wild boar hunted by his pack escaped him; and he has never once, in these deadly struggles, suffered the least injury, though his hounds have at times been fearfully wounded ".

No reference to the wild boar would be complete without some details concerning pig-sticking I do not know if it is the absolute record, but the following are the details of the most productive meet of which I have knowledge. On January 29th and 30th, 1906, at Moescoondie, 17 spears accounted for 149 boar. Malcolm Crawford was the host and organizer at this memorable meet, and from a detailed account which appeared in " The Field ", written by one of the participants, I take the following extracts : " Moescoondie is, or was—for it may have been washed away during the last eighteen years of inundations of the river—an island in the Ganges in Lower Bengal, about twelve miles long by three wide. At first it was covered with the grass and jhow jungle which is peculiar to rivers in India. Then cultivation was started on it. At first it was impossible to get the ryots to tackle it, as after the jungle had been cleared in patches with infinite toil the pig came out and destroyed all the crops, but by degrees the jungle was pushed back until it was small enough to be beaten, and in 1906 the island was at its best from a hunting point of view. ..... The plan of action was simple. The spears were divided into parties of three. The patches of jungle were enormous and the line was made up of 200 men with Crawford himself in charge, ably backed by Billy Barker and his assistants from the outlying factories. Most of the parties rode with the line, but some of them were posted outside the jungle. The line was most skilfully worked and there were no gaps in it, but for some time nothing showed. Then a few smallish pig began to break across the plain towards the next cover, and suddenly the plain was black with hundreds of pig of every size making their way across the open. Never have I seen such a sight! Portly matrons, followed by strings of striped piglings no bigger than rabbits; young boars, still showing the brown coat of the yearling, 26 in. pig, black as night, quick on their feet, more ready to run than to fight; and then the lords of the harem, ploughing their way through the press like great galleons, shouldering the smaller fry to right and left. Truly a sight to dream of, but only to be seen once in a life-time!

" All idea of parties was forgotten. Each man

picked his boar, let in the spurs and rode him, the trouble being to avoid the smaller pig, which were continually getting in the way.

" George Paris was brought down like this by a crossing pig early in the day, and retired with concussion and a cheek split from chin to ear, so that the subsequent proceedings interested him no more. ˙

" It was no place for children. In the open the odds were in favour of horse and man, but in cover it was different. The grass and jhow was almost up to the waist of a mounted man, and a hunted boar had a habit of squatting so that the rider overshot the mark, and the boar charged in behind. The going was quite blind and full of holes, and the only thing to do was to leave the horse's head alone, harden one's heart and drive him through it. The man who pulled rein and rode with caution always met with disaster."

" Most of the men and horses knew the game and could be backed to ride and kill their quarry single-handed, but that was not the only reason for the tremendous bag of 149 boar killed in the two days. The main reason was that these magnificent hog seemed to prefer to fight than to run, and most of them were killed after a quarter of a mile burst. Men whose names are famous in the annals of the Kadir and up-country hunts, like Medlicott of Skinner's Horse, and Pritchard, of the 2nd Lancers, have told me that though they have ridden many boar, they have never met anything to equal for undaunted courage the great grey boar of Moescoondie, who turns on his pursuer unwounded and almost unridden, full of the lust of battle, and charges home reckless of life, as ready to kill as to be killed."

On the first day three men tied with ten boar apiece to their credit, the total bag being 76 head, and on the second day 73 more were accounted for to make up the huge total of 149 for the two days.

CHAPTER XI

RED DEER

FROM time immemorial the red deer stag has been the supreme object of the chase throughout Europe, and to some of the privileged minority who enjoyed the right of the chase in the middle ages, the red stag was the passion of their lives. Since the death penalty could be enforced for acts of poaching, it can with truth be said that the life of a stag counted for more than the life of a man. In one case men were bartered for the horns of a stag, as history relates that a company of tall Grenadiers was given in exchange for the great sixty-six pointer shot in 1696 by the Elector Frederick III of Brandenburg, and we are also told that the refusal of the crown of Bohemia by the Elector John George. was not so much due to reasons of State as to the fact that the Bohemian stags were inferior both in numbers and size. Wars, rebellions, fires and other troubles have taken toll of some of the great collections of trophies that have come down to us, but some still exist in which the trophies are to be counted not by the hundred but by the thousand. At Moritzburg is preserved the finest collection of antlers in the world, and this is but a portion of the original, since Augustusburg, which housed the pick of the collection, was completely destroyed by fire early in the eighteenth century. The majority of the best heads at Moritzburg were weeded out from Augustusburg in 1725, so one can only speculate as to the treasures that the latter must have contained. In Moritzburg hang the largest pair of antlers known. This mighty head has a span of 75½ inches, but of its origin we know nothing, since its history cannot be traced further back than 1586, in which year it is enumerated in an inventory of the Elector Augustus's heirlooms. There were indeed giants in those days, and the great heads that hang in this old castle are magnificent memorials of hunting in mediæval Europe.

Modern methods of shooting are too well understood to call for comment, but in dealing with the records of the sport it is convenient to keep the Continental and Scottish statistics separate, whilst some notes concerning sport with the acclimatized deer of New Zealand will be found at the end of the chapter.

RED DEER

There can be little doubt that the man who killed the greatest number of red deer in all history was the Elector John George II of Saxony, whose bag amounted to the truly amazing total of 43,649, whilst his father John George I, whose reign was greatly disturbed by wars, accounted for 35,421 red deer.*

The largest number of deer bagged in a single Continental hunt that I can find recorded is 672 stags which were killed at a court battue in 1613.†

The two Electors of Saxony mentioned above were probably the greatest slaughterers of big game in the whole history of shooting, but before discussing their astonishing careers tribute must be paid to the work of W. A. Baillie-Grohman, whose knowledge of European sport was perhaps unrivalled by any other Englishman. Exhaustive research among private archives and in the state libraries of Vienna, Dresden, Munich, Gotha, Stuttgart, etc., yielded a quantity of historical matter of the utmost interest, and it is largely from his writings that the figures and substance of the following notes are taken.

* W. A. Baillee-Grohman : " Sport in the Alps " : 1896 : p 170.
† ibid. p. 177 (the locality is not stated).

163

BIG GAME SHOOTING RECORDS

THE ELECTORS JOHN GEORGE I AND II OF SAXONY
REIGNED 1611-1656 AND 1656-1680.

The following summary of game killed by these two mighty hunters was compiled from reliable sources by W. A. Baillie-Grohman.

	Elector John George I.	Elector John George II	Total of both.
Red deer ...	35,421	43,649	79,070
Fallow deer ...	1,045	2,062	3,107
Roe-deer ...	11,489	16,864	28,353
Total of deer	47,955	62,575	110,530
Wild boar ...	31,902	22,298	54,200
Bear ...	238	239	477
Wolves ...	3,872	2,195	6,067
Lynx ...	217	191	408
Hares ...	12,047	16,966	29,013
Foxes ...	19,015	2,740	21,755
Beavers ...	37	597	634
Badgers ...	930	1,045	1,975
Otters ...	81	180	261
Wild cats ...	149	292	441

Concerning these figures, Baillie-Grohman makes the following comments: " In Elector John George I's own MS. Hunting Diary, two gorgeously bound volumes, in part illuminated, preserved in the Dresden Royal Library, there is a complete list of all game caught, shot, and chased by this great hunter. It gives the total of deer at 47,239 head,* while Sylvanus, from whom the above lists are taken, gives a total of 47,955 head. How this discrepancy arose it would be difficult to say. There is another and more serious discrepancy in the number of bears and wolves. The former state that the father killed only 102 bears and 818 wolves, while Sylvanus gives the figures as 238 bears and 3,872 wolves. This probably arises from the fact that the former is the number killed by the Elector with his own hands, the latter those that were killed by the whole court personage. Tänzer, who wrote about the beginning of the following century, is very particular in saying that the deer were killed by the Elector John George I himself."

These enormous bags of game are all the more remarkable when it is remembered that they were made at a time when firearms were of a fearfully cumbersome nature. The personal equipment of the Electors, consisting of guns, powder horns, game bags, etc., has been exhibited at Continental hunting exhibitions. What their weapons lacked in handiness and range was made up for by the elaborate methods of driving the game. Miles of

* Of which 24,563 were stags.

BIG GAME SHOOTING RECORDS

palisades and the services of hundreds of beaters ensured the game being brought to within reasonable range.

Ths heaviest of the properly authenticated stags killed by the Electors was a beast shot on the 17th August, 1646, which weighed 61 stone 11 lbs., presumably as he stood, and 59 of the elder Elector's harts exceeded 56 stone.

No less remarkable than the weights of the stags were the horns that some of them carried as the following table shows:—

The finest antlers obtained by	John George I.	John George II.
Head of 30 points ...	1	
„ 28 „ ...	1	
„ 26 „ ...	1	
„ 24 „ ...	3	
„ 22 „ ...	9	6
„ 20 „ ...	25	26
„ 18 „ ...	133	54
„ 16 „ ...	374	295
„ 14 „ ...	1,202	985
„ 12 „ ...	3,147	2,108

Baillie-Grohman states that "the Electors of Saxony, owing to their ancient hereditary dignity of 'Lord High Masters of the Chase' to the Holy Roman Empire, enjoyed since 1350 exceptional opportunities to hunt, for this dignity gave them the right to exercise the rights of the chase in districts outside the confines of Saxony, which were 'Reichsunmittelbar', viz., which owed allegiance directly and only to the Emperor of Germany. In 1665, John George II rebuilt at vast cost a high palisade fence along the whole boundary between Saxony and Bohemia, so that his stags could not stray. The Elector Augustus had in the preceding century erected this immense fence, but it had fallen into disrepair ".

An interesting series of letters written by John George I to the Emperor Ferdinand was formerly preserved in the private archives of the Imperial family at Vienna. Concerning this interesting correspondence, Baillie-Grohman informs us that " thousands of stags are enumerated therein; the exact date and place where the heaviest were shot, what they weighed, and in the case of many of the larger ones the Elector even gives, by a line drawn on the margin of the paper, the so-called 'line of pride', representing the actual thickness of the layer of fat on the stag's haunches, and, now and again, also a second line indicating the thickness of the fat on the beast's brisket. Some of the former obtained from stags killed in the 'pride of grease', i.e., in the month preceding the rut, when the animals are in the best condition, measure over 4 inches ".

Other early hunting diaries and MSS. have yielded some astonishing records. The Landgrave John George of Brandenburg, when writing to the Landgrave of Hesse, gives him details of his bag for the past year (1581) as consisting of 677 stags, 968 hinds, and 501 wild boar. It was a Landgrave of Hesse who, so we are told, insisted on substituting in the Lord's Prayer an entreaty to " Give us our daily hart in the pride of grease". " The Dukes of Würtemberg were also great deer-hunters; thus Eberhard III of that ilk stalked during the rut of 1655 in eight days in a single forest, that of Urach, one stag of twenty points, one of eighteen points, seven of sixteen and fourteen points, and six of twelve and ten points; while his successor, Duke Eberhard Louis, in the same period bagged one stag of twenty-two points, one of eighteen points, eight of sixteen points, and sixteen of fourteen points, not to mention the stags of lesser heads, of which in both instances a number were killed."

Empresses and duchesses of those far off days were equally keen in the pursuit of the hart. It is recorded that Princess Frederica of Eisenach, who was noted for her skill in deer-stalking, shot on 21st August, 1693, in the Pillnitz Forest, a stag of twenty-six points, which scaled 60 stone 10 lbs., and was even then a remarkable weight, whilst Maria,

Governess of the Netherlands, could not only track her stag and bring him down with her cross-bow, but in the end could also gralloch her fallen quarry.

In France the chase was the all-absorbing subject until the outbreak of the Revolution. According to Le Comte Edouard Guy du Passage,* Louis XV, on his way back from his coronation at Reims, " drove in a carriage to his first hunt, in the Villers-Cotterets Forest, on St. Hubert's Day, 1722 . . . . . The King gave himself up to his hunting with all the eagerness of youth. François Mouret, his valet—who rode behind the King at every hunt carrying a wallet with a change of clothes—tells us that in 1725 the King hunted 276 days, was present at 362 kills, and rode 3,121 leagues. From 1743 to 1767, the kills by the Great Pack alone amounted to 2,651 stags. The Great Pack had from forty to ninety couples of different breeds, namely, the Norman breed, with a grey coat; mongrels resulting from a cross between English dogs and Norman or Vendée bitches; and English foxhounds. The number of the latter increased every year, for Louis XV kept on buying them, since, as years went on, the King required more and more speed from his pack. St. Hubert dogs acted as bloodhounds . . . . .

" The wild-boar hunting train and those of the

* " Country Life " : 8th December 1923.

wolf, roebuck and deer—the latter known as the Green Hunt, which was placed under the direction of M. de Dampierre and given to Mesdames the King's daughters—included a staff of more than five hundred noblemen, each of them being on duty for three months at a time. Two hundred and fifty horses were exclusively appropriated to the use of the Great Pack, fifty to the Wild-Boar Hunt, and a hundred to the others. The grand Ecuries, where two thousand horses were stabled, provided the courtiers or the King's guests with mounts."

His successor to the throne was an equally enthusiastic sportsman.

With the storming of the Bastille on the 14th July, 1789, it might be expected that the diary of Louis XVI would contain some reference to that day's happenings. The sole entry, however, is " killed nothing ", whilst on the 5th of the following October, the day on which the hordes of " Great Unwashed " hurled themselves upon Versailles, the only entry is as follows : " Shot at the gate of Chatillon, killed 81 head, interrupted by events; went and returned on horseback."

Modern bags appear insignificant in comparison with the huge totals of the seventeenth century, but it is interesting to note that the record bag of red deer in the nineteenth century stands to the credit of a descendant of the great Elector

RED DEER

of Saxony with whom we have already dealt. The bag of Duke Ernest II of Saxe-Coburg-Gotha is, so far as I have been able to trace, the record of modern times. Between 1837 and 1886 the Duke shot 3,283 red deer, of which 2,316 were stags.*

H.R.H. DUKE ERNEST II OF SAXE-COBURG-GOTHA

Springing from a dynastic race distinguished for its devotion to the chase, and as owner of some of the finest shooting in Europe, this great sportsman prince is one of the most notable figures in the history of continental sport.

Described as of knightly bearing and with the frame of a Hercules, his ideas on sport were in close accord with English views, and he was without doubt one of the most brilliant rifle shots of his own or any other day.

His bag of 3,283 red deer is unlikely ever again to be equalled, and of the 2,316 stags that he shot were one of 24 points, two of 22, four of 20, eight of 18, and 164 of 16 and 14 points.†

Mr. W. A. Baillie-Grohman, who was privileged to be his guest on many occasions, says that " as the Duke was in the habit of annually visiting all his sporting estates, and was, moreover, a frequent guest at the shooting parties of royal kinsmen, every day of the season was carefully

* Badminton Library : " Big Game Shooting : Vol. II : p. 113.
† NOTE.—These figures do not include what he shot between 1887 and 1893, the year that he died.

planned out months before. The year began for
him, as he would say, with a three weeks' visit
to Tyrol, where the season for chamois opens on
15th July. On returning to his Thuringian forests
he usually devoted the four weeks following the
15th August to his deer, their antlers being then
' clean ', and the animals themselves in perfect
condition. As stalking at that season of the year
is, of course, impossible in dense forest, driving
had to be resorted to, and for this purpose the
ground was divided into districts separated by
avenue-like cuttings through the forest, in which
the guns were posted . . . . . As the rides were
narrow, and stags invariably ' rush ' these open
spaces, the shooting was not the easiest. The
Duke generally occupied a Hochstand, i.e., a plat-
form raised some 8 or 10 feet over the ground,
from which elevation he, of course, commanded
a wider field. The Thuringian stags, though in
size nothing like to the Hungarian red deer, are
considerably larger animals than the Scotch deer,
and carry finer heads. In the fifty-six years in
which the Duke shot these forests, he killed seven
stags of from twenty to twenty-four points, and
over 200 of from fourteen to eighteen points. He
was one of the finest game shots with the rifle I
have ever met with, and he used to make some
marvellous shots with his favourite .450 Henry

Express. Thus I saw him once get a right and left across a valley at two deer in full flight. Some discussion arising as to the distance, he ordered it to be measured, and it was found to be 440 metres, or about 480 yards.

" On one occasion, when he was the guest of the old Emperor of Germany in the well-stocked forests of Letzlingen, the host was prevented by indisposition from going out, and the Duke, as the oldest royal personage present, was given the post usually occupied by the Emperor. The drive lasted three hours, and, when it was over, thirty-two stags were found lying in front of the Duke's ' stand '. What was remarkable about it was that every stag, however speedy the rush of the animal may have been, had been laid low by the ' master shot ' through the shoulder, just over the heart . . . . . On another occasion, a few years before, when driving the Inselberg in the Thuringian forest, the Duke with two double shots killed four stags (three of them of fourteen points) while in full flight, the first being over 200 yards off."

The following are interesting details of the Duke's bag during the last year that Baillie-Grohman was his guest, and no doubt the figures are fairly typical of all the later years of his life : " August 16th to September 15th, in Thuringia, 82 stags, 18 hinds; September 21st to October 31st, in Hinter-

Riss, Tyrol, 48 stags and 149 chamois; November 3rd to 7th, Wallersee in Upper Austria, 115 boars, and between 4 guns, 22 roebucks, 132 hares, 1,113 pheasants, 2 woodcock, and 6 partridges ".

He always spent the rutting season quite alone and so intensely fond of deer-stalking was he " that even during the very last season which he lived to see, he succeeded in killing several stags. He managed this by having himself drawn up in a sort of chair on wheels, before dawn of day, to the vicinity of the spot where the stag was calling, and doing the last bit of stalking on foot as best he could ".   Less than an hour before the fatal attack of apoplexy, " his master hand had brought down two royals! " and the last words that he is reported to have uttered were: " Let the drive commence! "

The Imperial forest of Spala in Poland was formerly one of the best stocked forests in Europe, and the low and undulating nature of the country made the sport comparatively easy. The Emperor of Russia and his guests used to shoot over this ground once a year when both driving and stalking were employed. The following are the details of the bag for 1900, made between 13th and 27th September, though unfortunately the number of guns is not stated.*

* Jean Stolzmann : in litt. 12th December 1900.

RED DEER

Stags killed by stalking

Heads of 20 points ...			1
„	18	„ ...	1
„	16	„ ...	8
„	14	„ ...	22
„	12	„ ...	29
„	10	„ ...	23
„	8	„ ...	1
„	6	„ ...	1

— 86 Stags.

Stags killed by driving

Heads of 14 points ...			7
„	12	„ ...	21
„	10	„ ...	25
„	8	„ ...	6
„	6	„ ...	1
„	4	„ ..	1
Brockets			1
Abnormal heads ...			2

— 64 Stags.

Hinds killed by driving	20
Total of Red Deer	170
Roedeer	44
Wild Boar	74
Foxes, Hares, and Winged Game ...	65
Total of all game	353

BIG GAME SHOOTING RECORDS

Some of the finest deer-stalking of modern times for both quality and quantity has been obtained at Munkacs in Hungary. This vast estate covers nearly 600 square miles, of which over half is forest. During the rutting season of 1894 or 1895 Count Schönborn and his guests shot the following stags:—

One of 18 points, three of 16, nine of 14, six of 12, six of 10, and three of 8 points.* On this same estate, according to E. von Dombrowski, a stag weighing 44 stone 4 lbs. clean has been obtained.

The annual yield of game of all sorts from certain of these vast Continental estates is enormous. In 1908 the total bag on the domain of the princely house of Schwarzenberg amounted to 78,900 head. This huge total included 1,529 deer, 84 fallow-deer, 48 chamois, 8 moufflon, 3,771 pheasants, 151 wild geese, 5,872 duck, 152 snipe, 23,921 hares, 1,428 rabbits, etc.†

The bags obtained in Spain do not compare with those of central Europe, but it is worthy of note that in the Coto Doñana preserve, during three and a half days' shooting in January, 1923, the guns (averaging twenty) accounted for 101 head of big game, comprising 42 red stags, 17 fallow deer, 39 wild boar, and 3 beasts of prey.‡

* W. A. Baillie-Grohman : " Sport in the Alps " : 1896 : p. 245.
† H. S. Gladstone : " Record Bags and Shooting Records " : 1922 : p. 126.
‡ Extract from Spanish Newspaper, quoted in " The Field " : 1923.

RED DEER

SCOTTISH RECORDS

Red deer were far less plentiful in Scotland in the middle ages than they are to-day, yet great bags were sometimes made by the methods of hunting then employed. One, William Barclay, of the court of Queen Mary has left us an account of a great drive in 1564. Two thousand Highlanders drove in the woods and hills of Atholl, Badenoch, Mar, and Murray, and two thousand red deer were brought within view of the Queen. The actual drive seems to have lasted for two months, but in a single day no less than 360 deer, 5 wolves, and some roe-deer were killed,* and this may well be the greatest number of deer ever killed in a day in Scotland.

Details of another Royal hunt in 1529 are given by Robert Lindsay of Pitscottie, in "The Chronicles of Scotland". On this occasion the Earl of Athole entertained King James V to three days' hunting, in the course of which 600 red deer together with roe-deer, wolves, foxes, etc., were slain.

At these great hunts the deer were mobbed by scores of men and dogs and all manner of weapons, including dirks and daggers, were used for their destruction.

* Quoted by J G. Millais in " The Mammals of Great Britain and Ireland " : 1906 : Vol. III : p 114 : from " De Regno et Regali Protestate adversus Monarchomachos ", which was translated from the Latin by Pennant.

Throughout the period of the cross-bow and long-bow, driving was the only method employed to kill deer, and even after the advent of fire-arms it continued to prevail until 1745. In modern times it is only at the end of the season and in the largest forests that it is practised. Mr. J. G. Millais gives the following particulars of a notable bag obtained by these means: "In the great extent of country formerly rented by the late Mr. Winans in Ross-shire, forty-six stags were shot by the tenant and his two sons in one day ".*

A remarkable incident in connection with stalking has been recorded by Mr. J. G. Millais† : On the 17th August, 1876, that noted shot, Mr. Walter Winans, killed 11 stags as the result of one stalk in the Danie Beat of Glen Strathfarrer, Inverness-shire, and, as Mr. Millais comments, not the least extraordinary part of the affair was, that there should have been eleven "shootable" beasts together in a party of fourteen stags.

Another noteworthy feat of stalking concerns the great Horatio Ross and his sons, an account of which was contained in an article over the signature of " A. Ross " in the " Shooting Times and British Sportsman " for December 5th, 1925, a portion of which was quoted in " The Field "

* " The Mammals of Great Britain and Ireland " : 1906 : Vol. III : pp. 132/3.
† ibid. p. 133.

of December 31st, 1925. From this I take the following: " In the forest of Dibidale, and in that part of Glendibidale which has for 40 years been reverenced as the Sanctuary, Capt. Ross and his sons made some remarkable shots at stags, and on one occasion they had a stalk at a bunch of eight stags on the south side of the glen. The weapons used were double-barrelled muzzle-loading Purdeys, and, of course, they could not reload and fire again. They fired their eight shots, and actually killed the eight stags. In those days stags were fewer in number, but the heads were much better than now. I am sure that Capt. Ross's eldest son, Edward, was a better rifle shot even than his celebrated father. He killed deer with the muzzle-loader at distances that his father would never have thought of shooting at them, and he won the Queen's Prize at Wimbledon the first year it was competed for, with the Enfield. He was tenant of Lord Lovat's forest of Glendoe for many years, that beautiful Inverness-shire preserve now the property of Mr. Noble. He was tall and athletic, but not so strongly built as his father, and he was a comparatively young man when he died ".

Capt. Horatio Ross was born in 1801 and lived till 1886 and he will always be remembered as one of the most remarkable shots with rifle, gun, or pistol that have ever lived. On his 80th birthday he shot two stags with a right and left, the latter being over 200 yards away,* and on December 20th, 1881, when in his 81st year, he fired twelve shots at a target with a 2-inch bull's-eye at 50 yards range. Seven of the shots were in the bull and the whole twelve were within a 3-inch circle. On May 15th of the following year, shooting with a rook-rifle, made by Holland and Holland, he fired eighteen shots at 100 yards range, seventeen of which were within a circle 5 inch in diameter.† Of his ability with the shotgun two instances may be quoted: On the 12th August, 1892, he is said to have killed 83 grouse in 83 shots, shooting over dogs,‡ and in June, 1828, shooting in a pigeon match he killed 79 birds out of 80 at 30 yards rise, thereby winning the match and defeating such noted shots as Lord Kennedy, Lord Anson, the Hon. Henry Moreton, the Hon. Twisselton Fiennes, Mr. Osbaldeston, Mr. Delmé Radcliffe, Capt. Delmé, Capt George Bentinck, Mr. Cruickshank, Mr. Anderson, Capt. Hall, Mr. Dare, Mr. Chinnery and Capt. Dickson.§

* " Ross-shire Journal ": 16th September 1881 (quoted in " The Field ", 15th April 1926).
† " The Field ": 15th April 1926.
‡ George Malcolm and Aymer Maxwell: " Grouse and Grouse Moors ": 1910: p. 271.
§ " The Field ": 21st January 1926.

RED DEER

The greatest number of stags ever killed in any Highland forest in a single season is, I think, 157, which number was obtained in the " Blackmount " as long ago as 1864,* but records of this nature are of no very great interest unless the quality of the heads and the weights are also known.   In 1895, in Strathraick, Mr. John Williams killed 105 stags which included one thirteen pointer and ten royals,† whilst few, if any forests, show a higher standard of excellence than Langwell and Braemore, where the Duke of Portland has I think had fifty seasons.   In 1925, 107 stags from this ground averaged 15 stone 5 lbs., the heaviest weighed 23 stone 4 lbs., and there were four others over 20 stone; 1 thirteen pointer, 5 royals, and 5 eleven pointers were among those killed and the best royal had the following dimensions: length 36 inches, beam 5⅛ inches, span 30½ inches.   In 1929, 103 stags were killed with an average weight of 15 stone 7 lbs. (clean); the heaviest was 24 stone 10 lbs., and no less than 14 weighed over 20 stone.   Included among the heads were 1 thirteen pointer and 5 royals, the best royal being 38⅝ inches in length, and in 1930 the four best heads were 2 fourteen pointers, a

* J. G. Millais : " The Mammals of Great Britain and Ireland " : 1906 : Vol. III : p. 130.

† Ibid. p. 131.

thirteen pointer, and a royal, all of which measured from 30 to 36¼ inches in length.*

The question of who has shot the greatest number of deer in Scotland I am unable to answer with absolute certainty, but I am inclined to think that Lord Desborough with a total of some 1,300 stags has killed the most.†

I quote the following from some interesting notes that Lord Desborough has kindly furnished me with: "I have done a certain amount of shooting big game in India, Africa, and the Rocky Mountains, and secured some good specimens. As regards deer-stalking in Scotland, it requires more art than shooting of wild game, as the less animals have seen of man the easier they are to get at. I have killed some thirteen hundred stags in Scotland, and have had glorious long days on the hill; there is nothing so attractive as the wild corries of Scotland used to be, and when one was young one could not get tired ".

In thirty-two seasons ending 1921, Mr. Sydney Loder killed 1,173 stags, all of which were killed by stalking.‡ His brother, Sir Edmund Loder, a noted shot and big game hunter was also an

---

* " The Field " : 8th January 1925 : 25th January 1930 : 4th April 1931.
† Lord D. *in litt.* 30th June 1931.
‡ Sir Alfred E. Pease : " Edmund Loder—A Memoir " : 1923 : p. 86.

enthusiastic deer-stalker. Between 1894 and 1915
his total amounted to 420, but this number includes some chamois.*

There are, I think, one or two other men now
living who have killed over a thousand stags in
Scotland but I am unable to give exact statistics.

NEW ZEALAND RECORDS

History affords ample proof that the transfer
of wild animals to a new and strange environment
is an experiment, the results of which are at all
times uncertain. The liberation of non-indig-
enous animals in unenclosed country is liable to
disturb the balance of nature and to have far-
reaching and unforeseen results. The acclimatization of Scottish and English red deer in New
Zealand has proved no exception, though its
problems are not to be compared with the difficulties arising out of the introduction of the rabbit
in Australia.

For many years the New Zealand herds of deer
were allowed to increase unchecked. The best
deer spread outward from the main herds which
in time became composed of rubbish of both
sexes. In 1923 it was estimated that the deer
totalled 300,000 head and in the more settled
parts of the Dominion they had become a menace

* Sir Alfred E. Pease : " Edmund Loder—A Memoir " : 1923 :
p. 274.

to agriculture. In this year a permit was granted to Mr. J. G. Sutherland, a farmer of Pirinoa, Wairarapa, to shoot red deer, and he reported to the Wellington Acclimatization Society that he had shot 667 deer in five days, the largest number for one day being 194.*

Since then, much has been done to control their numbers, but it is not so much with figures connected with the mere reduction of the herds that we are concerned as with the results obtained by the deer-stalker in the pursuit of the big heads. In spite of the deterioration caused by overcrowding, magnificent trophies are still to be obtained by penetrating into the rough and remote country in which the best deer are to be found.

For quality and quantity it is probable that the best bag ever brought out of New Zealand as the result of one season's stalking was obtained by Lord and Lady Belper in 1925. This trip was made in the Otago country where the deer are descendants of Scottish stock obtained from Invermark and liberated in 1870.

The following are the measurements of the seven magnificent heads obtained. Numbers 3 and 7 were shot by Lady Belper and the remainder by Lord Belper.†

* " The Field " : 4th October 1923.
† Ibid. 6th August 1925.

184

RED DEER

No.	*Points.*	*Length.*	*Beam.*	*Span.*	*Spread.*
1	8+8	48	6¾	33¾	41
2	7+7	45½	6	31½	41
3	7+6	44¾	5	27	34¼
4	6+6	44½	6¼	31¾	40¼
5	6+6	40¾	5½	28¼	35
6	6+6	38½	5½	33½	42¾
7	8+7	38	5¾	28½	36¼

No. 1 is certainly one of the finest, if not the finest, head ever killed in Otago, and the skull weighed 25 lbs. before it was boiled.

CHAPTER XII

ROE-DEER

IN this chapter I refer only to the European roe (*Capreolus caprea*) and not to the larger Asiatic varieties of this animal.

Taking Europe as a whole, there are probably seven roebucks killed to every one stag, and in an average year prior to the Great War nearly 100,000 roe-deer were killed in Austria alone, whilst in Germany some 200,000 were shot annually. On the Continent the roe is held in far greater esteem than in Scotland and England, and to some well-known Continental sportsmen the roebuck has been their ruling passion. One has but to see some of the great private collections to realise the amount of interest taken in this sporting little animal. The famous collection of Count Arco-Zinneberg contains over 2,300 trophies, and nearly £300 is said to have been paid by this ardent collector for one small though curiously malformed head.

The prizes awarded for roe heads at the Continental exhibitions of trophies are among the most coveted honours to be won, and, at the International Shooting and Field Sports Exhibition at Vienna in 1910, the collection prize for roe went to Prince Charles Trauttmansdorf who exhibited a group of 103 splendid heads from his collection.

In France, where the roe has for centuries been hunted by hounds, it is the sole quarry of many packs, and partly the quarry of some dozens of others. Taking Europe as a whole, however, it is probably true to say that the rifle accounts for considerably more than half the number killed. Stalking, or still-hunting, with the rifle, is usually regarded as the highest form of sport that the roe-deer affords, but in Scotland this method is only practised by a minority and they are more commonly killed with shot guns at autumn and winter covert shoots.

In Germany a popular way of shooting the buck is by calling him in the rutting season. The cry of the doe can be imitated by blowing in a particular manner on beech or hazel leaves and artificial calls are also manufactured.

From a study of European records it is evident that the roe-deer is more plentiful to-day than it was in the middle-ages, and its horns show no such deterioration as has occurred in the case of the red deer.

BIG GAME SHOOTING RECORDS

In detailing bags of roe it is essential to state how they were obtained : whether by driving or stalking and whether with rifle or shot gun; without such particulars the figures can be of but little interest.

In spite of the fact that the roe-deer were not so plentiful in Europe in former times as they are to-day, there can be little doubt that the Elector John George II, who occupied the throne of Saxony from 1656 to 1680, killed more of these animals than any other man. According to reliable sources, of which I have given details in Capter XI, he killed no less than 16,864 roe, whilst his father Elector John George I, who reigned from 1611 to 1656, killed 11,489.

Two historical records of considerable interest are mentioned by W. A. Baillie-Grohman in " Sport in the Alps ". In 1545 Duke William IV of Bavaria killed 1,032 red deer, 535 wild boar, 38 wolves and 224 roe-deer, whilst in 1583 the Elector of Brandenburg killed 1,295 red deer and 249 roe-deer. In the course of a great deal of research undertaken by Baillie-Grohman in six-teenth-century annals, these two bags show the smallest preponderance of red deer over roe-deer. At this period ten red deer to one roe seems to have been the more usual proportion, with a gradual increase in the number of roes in the following two hundred years.

ROE-DEER

Turning to more recent times, the largest bag obtained in a single day's driving of which I have been able to find reliable reference is mentioned by J. G. Millais. He does not mention the date or the number of guns, but he writes as follows* :
" The late C. Macpherson Grant, who had the autumn shooting of Beaufort (Scotland) for two years, told me that he and his party in one day in Farley Wood, Beaufort, killed 65 roe, besides 13 hinds and 13 woodcock. Fifty have several times been killed in the same wood by the late Lord Lovat and his parties ".

Particulars of some other big days at Farley appeared in " The Field " of the 9th August, 1928. On the 18th November, 1887, the bag was 45, and on the 25th November, 1885, it amounted to 42.

Between 1830 and 1849, 56 roe were killed in one day at Monromon Moor, near Kinnaird Castle,† and 42 is the largest number killed in a day in Darnaway Forest.‡

It can be taken for granted that all these Scotch bags were obtained with shot guns.

On the Continent the largest bag of which I have knowledge was obtained in the Imperial lorest of Bialovieja,§ where the Emperor of

* " British Deer and their Horns " : 1897 : p. 174.
† H. S. Gladstone : " Record Bags and Shooting Records " : 1922 : p. 125.
‡ Lord M. in litt. 3rd December 1928.
§ Bialovieja, Bielovêge, or Bialowicza.

189

Russia formerly held an annual shoot. In this vast preserve 325 roebucks and 3 does, together with a large bag of bison, elk, red deer, wild boar, etc., were killed between August 31st and September 12th, 1900. As the full details of this enormous bag of big game are given in the chapter devoted to the European bison it is unnecessary to repeat them here.

In Count Joseph Potocki's forest of Schepetowka, Volhynia, ten rifles shot 77 roebucks and a hundred odd wild boar in four days' shooting in 1912.*

In Belgium, roe are fairly plentiful and they are mostly killed in battues. On the estate of Baron de Woot de Janée, during two days' driving, 1,800 head of game, which included 29 roe-deer, were killed.†

In the Ardennes, where roe and wild boar are the principal game animals, Mr. H. J. Elwes has recorded that he has known 28 roe and 11 pigs killed in one day's driving.‡ Elwes was a member of the Société de Bouillon, an old-established shooting syndicate. He does not mention the number of guns that accounted for this particular bag, but he states that the guns usually totalled ten or twelve.

* Count Roman Potocki : in litt. 15th April 1929.
† Henri Querain : " Sport in Europe " : 1901 : p. 90.
‡ " Memories of Travel, Sport, and Natural History " : 1930 : p. 141.

ROE-DEER

With regard to stalking with the rifle, the record bag appears to have been made in Hungary, where His Imperial and Royal Highness the Archduke Francis Ferdinand shot in the spring of 1899, 66 selected old bucks in three days on the estate of Count Tassilo Festetics.*

A notable day's sport was obtained by the Crown Prince Rudolf of Austria, who stalked and shot 18 roe in one morning at Keszthely,† and one day prior to the Great War, on the estates of Count Z. Tarnowski, at Dzikow, Polish Selicia, five rifles, shooting in the morning and evening, accounted for no less than 52 bucks.‡

Mr. J. G. Millais has given details in connection with a feat of roe-deer shooting which are extraordinary for more reasons than one; he says§:
" Roe exist in very large numbers on some of the islands of the Danube, for at the Vienna Exhibition of 1910 we were afforded the unique exhibition of 113 roebuck heads shot in nine days by a sportsman who not only showed the results of his prowess, but himself, suitably attired in hunting costume and clasping his rifle. . . . . . Most of these heads were killed from a canoe

* Géza Count Széchényi : " Sport in Europe " : 1901 : p. 61.
† Baron Donald Schönberg : " Sport in Europe " : 1901 : p. 156.
‡ Count Roman Potocki : in litt. 15th April 1929.
§ " The Gun at Home and Abroad " : Vol. III : 1914 : p. 314.

propelled by a keeper, whilst the shooter sat in the bows and picked off the best bucks as they fed on the water edge at morn or eve ".

In the south of Sweden, where some of the finest heads have been obtained, roe-deer were formally killed at battues together with hares, foxes, etc., but following the introduction of pheasants and rabbits they have, since the beginning of the present century, been more usually killed by stalking them with the rifle. By this method, Count Stig Thott informs me that he has shot as many as 12 in a single day's stalking.

A remarkable incident is mentioned in " The Badminton Magazine ", Vol. XXI, September, 1905, p. 244, and quoted by Mr. Hugh S. Gladstone in " Record Bags and Shooting Records " (1922). From the latter work I take the following : " It is recorded that at a battue at the Göhrde, not far from Hamburg, on 14th January, 1845, King Ernst August of Germany shot four roe-deer at one shot : doubtless with a bullet but still surely ' some record ' ".

CHAPTER XIII

CHAMOIS

WITH the one notable exception to which I shall presently refer, the hunters of the middle ages paid little attention to the pursuit of the chamois. To this deeply superstitious race of people all the dangers of Alpine life were attributed to occult powers. Avalanche, flood, lightning, and mist were alike regarded as the manifestations of the various spirits of the mountains, the fear of which undoubtedly retarded both sport and exploration throughout the great mountain chain which is the chamois' home. To such as followed it, the sport must have been of a most exacting nature, since to kill a chamois with no other weapon than a 9 or 10 foot javelin required climbing powers, and a knowledge of the ground and game, of which the modern Nimrod might well be proud. The gradual improvement in early firearms had but little effect on the sport of chamois hunting, since this coincided with the luxury and pageant loving ages of the 17th and 18th centuries, when an amusement of so stern a nature made but little appeal. The chase of the chamois, as it is understood to-day, may be said to date from the beginning of the 19th century, when the example of the Archduke John of Austria in stalking chamois was quickly followed by the upper classes. Since that time, chamois shooting, whether by stalking or driving, has maintained its position as one of the finest forms of sport that Europe offers.

The largest number of chamois ever killed in one day which I can find recorded is 183, and this enormous bag was obtained before the days of firearms. It was the result of a great drive held by the Emperor Maximilian (1459-1519) in the Schmirn mountains.* On such an occasion as this the inhabitants of all the nearest villages were commanded to act as beaters and the chamois were killed with javelins at an average range of perhaps 25 to 30 yards.

Before turning to more recent records a few words must be said concerning the Emperor Maximilian of Austria, who was one of the most adventurous, sport-loving and romantic figures of European history, and whose love of chamois hunting seems to have exceeded that of any other sport.

*" Sport in the Alps " : p. 12 (quoted from " Weisskunig ").

CHAMOIS

Our present knowledge of this great hunter is based on two printed works, namely, " Weiss-kunig " and " Theuerdank ", and on two manu-scripts, one of which is preserved in the Imperial Library in Vienna and the other in the Royal Library in Brussels. All four are considered to have been written or dictated by the Emperor. Both of the first-named works have been re-printed, but they are practically unknown in this country, and the best known references to the Emperor in the English language are to be found in the writings of W. A. Baillie-Grohman. From this great authority's " Sport in the Alps " I take the following extracts : Speaking of his skill with the long-bow, he says that he " was one of the few foreigners who proved himself equal to British archers in the handling of the long-bow, in the management of which the English, since the time of Edward III, were acknowledged by all nations to have been far and away the most skilled. Such strength had he in his arms, that as he him-self relates in the first-named work (Weisskunig), he once shot a wooden arrow, on which there was no iron whatever, through a plank of very hard larch wood 3 inches thick ". After referring at some length to the books and manuscripts I have already mentioned, he goes on to say : " These four works give one a fairly accurate idea of the manner in which the chase of the chamois was conducted by Maximilian, while some additional notes found in the archives at Innsbruck, the capital of the country, in which lay his favourite hunting-grounds, no less than some of his arms preserved in the Imperial Museum in Vienna, enable one to picture to oneself the personality of this bold climber and explorer of the mountain wilds ". He was one of the last sportsmen of great position who ordinarily used the cross-bow and " for big game, short arrows with massive iron points were used, while for small game lead bullets were preferred. Though, as a rule, different cross-bows were used for arrows and bullets, there were such that could be converted so as to use either. Maximilian must have been an excellent shot with this arm, for he shot ducks as they rose from the water, killing on one occasion 100 ducks with 104 shots. Once he killed 26 hares, without missing once, with one and the same arrow, though his biography does not mention how many of them were running shots. In winter, on account of great cold rendering steel dangerously brittle, Maximilian tells his successor he is to use in the chase of the chamois a cross-bow with a bow made of horn. The ' hand-gonne ' or fire-tube, as the first exceedingly primitive fire-arm used in the chase was called, was never used by the Emperor for chamois-hunting. . . . . In 'Weisskunig' there is narrated the following incident, proving the superiority of the cross-bow, when in such skilled hands as those of Maximilian, over the hand-gonne of his day. Maximilian, accompanied by one Yörg Purgkhardt, who is described as a man most skilled in the use of the fire-tube, went out chamois shooting. Coming upon a chamois standing high over their heads on a rock, the Emperor commanded Yörg to shoot the buck with his fire-tube, but the latter declared that the chamois was much too high up, and could not be reached by his bullet. Whereupon Maximilian, taking his cross-bow, said, ' Look-out, I shall kill that buck with my steel cross-bow,' and really brought him down the very first shot, the distance being 100 klafter, or over 200 yards.

" But the Emperor's favourite manner of hunting the chamois was with the javelin, which, of course, was far more difficult than with the cross-bow, for to be successful it was necessary to get to close quarters and tread the dangerous paths and narrow ledges to which the game, when pressed, always takes refuge. This sporting spirit of desiring to come to close quarters with his game distinguished Maximilian in a high degree.

The more dangerous the foe, the greater the zest with which this courageous sportsman entered the fray. Hand-to-hand personal encounters, in which the skill, strength, or endurance of the hunter vanquished the ferociousness or fleetness of foot of the hunted beast, were the joy of his life. Maximilian would journey afar to meet single-handed a great bear or monster boar that had been marked to cover for him. And what enormous sizes those beasts then still attained we know from game registers, that give their weights as up to 900 and 800 lbs. respectively."

" These beasts he would tackle on foot single-handed in their lair, armed either with the short hunting spear, with which, gripped firmly in both hands, the charge of the beast was received, or with his hunting sword or hanger." . . . . " With either in his hand he seems to have feared no beast, and his adventures were of the most thrilling kind. When on horseback in pursuit of a big stag he would, when the cornered beast turned and charged, receive the infuriated beast at the point of the latter arm. But of all these various modes of pursuing game that resulted in dangerous hand-to-hand combats with the fiercest beasts of prey, none, according to his own accounts, brought him so often into deadly peril as the chamois chase with the javelin, or Schaft, as was its technical term. Swiftly moving avalanches, showers of stones, set in motion by beaters or by the game itself, shot chamois tumbling down upon the sportsmen from heights above, rocks giving way, the snapping of his alpenstock, the giving way in a most dangerous place of five or six spikes of his crampon, slipping on narrow ledges and being saved from instant death by a quick leap into the top of a handy tree growing below, or, on another similar occasion, by clinging with one hand to a point of rock, are, one and all, adventures narrated by the Emperor "...... " Maximilian's sporting establishment was very large, consisting of Masters of the Chase, Master of the Forest, keepers and kennelmen by the hundred, for he had separate staffs in most of the Austrian provinces, and in his kennels were no fewer than 1,500 hounds. The latter were, however, chiefly used when other royal guests were present, to whom the hardships of stalking were less welcome than they were to Maximilian himself ".

I have referred earlier in the chapter to the great drive he held in which no less than 183 chamois were accounted for in a single day's sport, and there can be no doubt that he fully deserved to be acknowledged in the manner that he was—as the Master of the Masters of the Chase.

BIG GAME SHOOTING RECORDS

In modern times all the largest bags have, of course, been made by driving, and the record collective bag appears to have been obtained in the Zillerthal Alps, where, in the famous shoot of Prince Auersperg, 94 chamois were shot in one drive on August 31st, 1892, and the result of six days' driving was a total of 222 to five guns, only bucks and barren does being killed.* The vast preserve where this great bag was made was divided by its natural features into three divisions, each of which was left undisturbed for two years in succession.

Another bag of great magnitude was made in September, 1912, at a Royal shoot in the Picos de Europa in Spain. On the first day there were eleven guns and 81 chamois were killed.†

In 1897, during a day's driving on Mount Poucet, King Humbert of Italy shot 49 chamois out of a total bag of 69,‡ and this is the largest individual bag that I have found recorded, though according to Count Scheibler, His Majesty averaged 50 chamois a day during his annual visits to the Royal preserve in Val del Gesso. King Humbert was a first-rate shot, his

* Randolph L. Hodgson : " Big Game Shooting " (The " Country Life " Library of Sport) : 1905 : Vol. I : p. 137.

† Abel Chapman : " The Gun at Home and Abroad " : Vol. III : 1914 ; p. 380

‡ " The Field " : 11th September 1897.

favourite weapon being a .450 Express by Holland and Holland.

I cannot say with certainty who has shot the greatest number of chamois during a lifetime, but this record probably belongs to the Royal sportsman just mentioned, or to Duke Ernest II of Saxe-Coburg-Gotha, whose total was 2,000.* According to W. A. Baillie-Grohman the Duke's best season yielded 149, but it should be remembered that in his early days he shot his chamois by stalking, and it was only with advancing years that he took to driving. I have referred to his wonderful ability with the rifle in Chapter XI, and had he gone in for driving earlier his bag of chamois would have been even larger than it was.

Very few Englishmen have had an extensive experience of chamois shooting. Baillie-Grohman enjoyed the sport in many of the finest preserves in Europe, and Sir Edmund Loder rented good chamois ground from 1895 to 1897 and from 1905 to 1907, but to the great majority it is a little known sport.

Chamois hunting is also to be obtained in the Pyrenees, in Greece, and in the Caucasus, but I can find no record of any very large bags having been made in these countries.

* W. A. Baillie-Grohman : " Sport in the Alps " : 1896 : p. 62.

CHAPTER XIV

EUROPEAN BISON

THE European bison or zubr is sometimes referred to as the aurochs, though this name properly belongs to the urus, or wild ox, which has been extinct in Europe for several hundred years.

The European bison (*Bos bonassus*) is a creature of huge bulk and sometimes attains a height of over six feet at the shoulder. The enormous development of the fore-quarters appears to be exaggerated by the mass of brown hair with which the back of the head, neck, shoulders, and chest are covered, giving the animal a look of innate wildness.

Essentially forest-loving creatures, they are generally shy and retiring, though, according to Lydekker, an old bull has been known to take possession of a road in Lithuania and to challenge all comers.

Formerly abundant over a large area of Europe their range at the beginning of the present century was confined to Lithuania, where they were strictly preserved in the Imperial forest of Bielovêge,* to the Kouban district of the Caucasus, and to a small herd in Silesia on the property of the Prince of Pless. Political troubles, uprisings, and disturbances of a like nature have always proved detrimental to the bison, as such events have invariably resulted in poaching to a greater or less extent, and as the cows are only believed to calve once in three years, a strict measure of protection is essential to the maintenance of their numbers.

The bison formerly extended into Siberia, and E. Demidoff (Prince San Donato), in an interesting contribution to "Sport in Europe", mentions the report of a native hunter having seen three animals in the woods which he recognized as bison on being shown the illustration of one in a book of natural history. This cannot, of course, be accepted as evidence that they exist there, but it must be within the bounds of possibility that some herds still live in certain of the vast and unexplored forest areas of that little known country.

According to Mr. F. A. Lucas, the bison was common in Poland up to 1500, "where it was looked upon as royal game, and hunted in right royal manner by the King and nobility, as many as two thousand or three thousand beaters being

* Bielovêge, Bialovieja or Bialowicza.

employed to drive the game. In 1534 the animal was still so numerous in the vicinity of Girgau, Transylvania, that peasants passing through the woods were occasionally trampled to death by startled bison ". It is probable therefore that some very large bags were made at this period, but the largest I can find recorded is of considerably later date. According to the same authority a grand hunt was organized by the Polish King, Augustus III, in 1752, when 60 bison were killed in a single day.*

By 1815 the Lithuanian herd was estimated to contain no more than 300 head, but careful protection increased it to 700 by 1830, though a local revolt in the following year reduced its numbers to 637. An official enumeration took place at the end of each decade and by 1860 the total was 1,700. During the Polish uprising of 1863, however, they were killed in such numbers that the next official count amounted to only 847, and by 1880 the herd had waned to 600. I do not know at what date this great forest of Bielovêge was enclosed, but I believe it was in this state during the reign of the late Czar. Once a year the Emperor and his guests shot over a portion of the ground and some enormous bags of big game were obtained.

Quoted by R. Lydekker in " The Royal Natural History " 1894 : Vol. I : p. 190.

EUROPEAN BISON

The following is a complete list of the game killed between August 31st and September 12th. 1900:—

Bison . . .	42
Elk . . .	36
Red Deer (Stags) .	53
Deer (? Hinds) .	26
Roe-deer (Bucks) .	325
„ (Does) .	3
Wild Boar . .	138
Foxes . . .	51
Winged Game .	11
Total . .	685

The number of rifles that accounted for this vast total is not stated, but Prince Albert of Saxe-Altembourg killed the most, his figures being as follows: 12 bison, 37 stags, 39 roebucks, 16 other deer, 24 wild boar, 10 foxes, and 1 woodcock.*

I do not know whether the 42 bison in this bag is the absolute record for modern times, as these are the only exact figures that I have been able to obtain, but if they have been exceeded, it would not have been by very many, as according to E. Demidoff (Prince San Donato) thirty to forty was the average number shot.

* Jean Stoltzmann : *in litt.* 12th December 1900.

BIG GAME SHOOTING RECORDS

Very few Englishmen ever had the opportunity of shooting in these wonderful preserves. Major Algernon Heber Percy shot a bull and a cow bison, and in 1898 Mr. E. N. Buxton obtained some splendid photographs of bison, but I do not know whether he shot any specimens.

Of the few that existed in the Caucasus, only three were allowed to be shot annually, this being the self-imposed limit of the Grand Duke Serge whose Kouban preserves constituted their only stronghold. So far as I know the only Englishman who ever shot a bison in the Caucasus was St. George Littledale, who was virtually the discoverer of these animals in that country, the Kouban preserve being established at a later date.

ST. GEORGE LITTLEDALE

As a hunter of big game in the Northern Hemisphere, the name of Littledale must surely stand alone. His success in this sphere has never I think been equalled, most certainly never surpassed. During the course of his long and adventurous life he penetrated into many of the most inacessible regions, and obtained some of the rarest trophies that have ever fallen to the rifle of a hunter. In 1893 he carried out an important journey of exploration in which he crossed Asia from the Caspian to Peking. During this trip he mapped a large territory between Lob Nor and Koko Nor and in the regions of the Upper Hoangho, whilst in the two following years he accomplished the most difficult feat of crossing Tibet, but it is of his achievements as a hunter that we are here concerned.

It was in 1891 that he shot the two European bison (male and female) which he presented to the Natural History Museum, London, and so far as I know he still remains the only Englishman who has ever shot these rare beasts in the Caucasus, and at that time they lived in a perfectly wild and unprotected state. A long hunt in the previous year had proved fruitless, so that his success, when it came, had been well earned. It speaks volumes for his forbearance that he refrained from shooting a third and finer specimen. I quote his own words with regard to this incident* : " Some weeks after that, I found myself face to face with a grand old bull, bigger than my first victim. We were hidden in the bush and he stood in the open wood, and grand indeed he looked. I laid my rifle down, for the temptation was great, and I would not have slain him for £1,000. I took off my cap to him out of respect for a noble representative of a nearly extinct

* Badminton Library : " Big Game Shooting " : Vol. II.

species; I had got what I wanted, and mine should not be the hand to hurry further the extermination of a fading race for mere wanton sport". It would be hard to find a better example of true sportsmanship than that. As the two specimens he had already shot were destined for the National Collection the temptation to secure the third for himself must have been very great, but he yielded not, and those few lines from his pen are, I think, one of the finest passages in the whole literature of big game.

Magnificent trophies are to be won in the Caucasus, but it is a hard and difficult country where every shot has to be worked for. Littledale's success in this country was wonderful. On one occasion he obtained four splendid stags at one stalk. On this particular day he was lying on a ridge near the summit of the divide and within his view were " a dozen old male tur in an unstalkable position, two bears whose skins (it being August) were not worth having, a chamois scorned as small game, and the stags which he ultimately bagged ".* In 1887 his bag in the Caucasus amounted to 7 ollen or red deer stags, 7 ibex, 11 chamois, together with some bears and wild boar.

His best stag's head, and it is the record

* Badminton Library : " Big Game Shooting " : Vol. II

EUROPEAN BISON

with the exception of one owned by Mr. H. O. Whittal, has the following measurements: Length on outside curve, 47¼ in.; circumference, 7¼ in.; tip to tip, 33½ in.; widest inside, 43¼ in.; spread, 54¾ in.; points, 10+9.

In 1874 he was in the Rocky Mountains, and in two months' shooting he secured no less than 13 mountain sheep and some wapiti,* and at other times he visited Alaska, Colorado and Newfoundland.

In 1875 Littledale met Sir Edmund Loder in India which resulted in a life-long friendship between them. As an immediate result of this chance meeting they decided to visit the Neilgherry Hills together, and in fifteen days' shooting, Littledale's bag amounted to 7 ibex, 2 sambur stags and 1 hind.†

He visited the Pamirs of central Asia in 1888 when he shot 17 ovis poli, and again in 1890. A 62¼ in. head that he got was sent to Her Imperial Majesty the Czarevna, she having expressed a wish to have one of his trophies.‡

One of the results of his journey across Tibet was the obtaining of three specimens of the wild camel of which he brought home all the skins and skulls and one complete skeleton.

* "Edmund Loder" by Sir Alfred E. Pease : 1923 : p. 174.
† Ibid. p. 177.
‡ Badminton Library : "Big Game Shooting" : Vol. II.

209

BIG GAME SHOOTING RECORDS

Perhaps the most noteworthy trophy that Littledale ever obtained is the great Siberian argali head that he shot in the Altai. This magnificent trophy, which is the largest ever recorded by Rowland Ward, measures 62¼ ins. on the front curve and 19¾ ins. in circumference. Another great head that he obtained is that of an Asiatic ibex in the possession of H.M. the King. The measurements are: Length, 54 ins.; circumference, 10¾ ins.; tip to tip, 45 ins. At one time and another he also obtained outstanding trophies of the following: Carpathian stag, American wapiti, Asiatic wapiti, Newfoundland caribou, prongbuck, Siberian roebuck, Mongolian gazelle, chamois, Cashmere serow, Rocky Mountain goat, Caucasian ibex, Caucasian bharal, Palla's bharal, Ladak bharal, Colorado bighorn, Littledale's argali, Kobet Dagh urial, American bison, etc.

Littledale's skill with the rifle was of the very highest order. In his early days he used a double .500 Express, but with the advent of the small-bore high-velocity rifles he took to using the .256 Mannlicher, and he was probably one of the first three Englishmen to adopt this rifle for sporting purposes, the other two being Sir Edmund Loder and Sir Alfred Pease.

With one of these rifles, sighted and stocked by Gibbs of Bristol, which he was trying in 1897, he made a wonderful group. The clip of five shots was fired at 100 yards range and the group, which was in the dead centre of the target, is completely hidden if covered by a six-penny-piece. This classic target was reproduced in " The Book of the Rifle " and in " The Field " of May 23rd, 1931.

I had hoped to obtain some additional and first-hand information concerning the career of this great hunter and explorer, but before I was able to do so I learnt of his death. During his lifetime he gave many valuable specimens to the Natural History Museum, and now that he has left us he has bequeathed to the Nation all that is best in his magnificent collection of trophies.

CHAPTER XV

ELK

THE principal homes of the Elk in Europe are in Scandinavia, East Prussia, Poland, Lithuania, parts of Russia and eastwards into subarctic portions of Siberia where its extreme limits are not definitely known. Being essentially a forest animal its northern extension is governed by the presence of trees.

On some of the immense Continental estates belonging to crown or nobility, where the preservation of game is carried to a high degree, driving on a large scale is practised, and, in a small way, it is sometimes attempted in Norway by employing beaters to move the elk out of deep gorges or very thick woodlands towards the rifle or rifles. The more usual method of hunting the elk in Norway, however, is with the aid of an elk-dog in leash, patiently working up and across the wind to enable the dog to scent either the beast itself or its fresh spoor. In Sweden the dog is allowed to range loose in order that it may bring

ELK

the elk to bay or otherwise impede it till the
hunter can get up and obtain a shot. In Russia,
driving, tracking on snow-shoes, and calling the
elk during the rutting time are methods commonly adopted.

A bull elk of the first class may stand six feet
or over at the withers, and heads with a span of
over 50 inches are recorded.

The largest bags have naturally been obtained
where the game is strictly preserved and driving
is practised.

So far as I can ascertain the record bag of elk
for a single day's driving was made in Sweden.
I am greatly indebted to the authorities of the
Royal Hunt for their courtesy in furnishing me
with, and allowing me to publish, details of the
bags which have been obtained at the Royal elk-
shooting parties on Hunneberg and Halleberg.

" At a shooting party in 1885, in which the
Prince of Wales took part, 73 elk were killed in
one day by about 30 rifles."

" The mountains of Halleberg and Hunneberg
are situated on the south shore of Lake Wenern
in Westergötland. The surface of this Royal
preserve is about 14,000 acres. The shooting
parties lasting two days take place every second
year and the number of rifles is about 15. The

following bags have been obtained in the last ten years ": —

    1921 :   14 bulls, 11 cows, total 25 elk.
    1924 :   33 bulls, 10 cows, ,,   43 elk.
    1926 :   20 bulls, 15 cows, ,,   35 elk.
    1928 :   14 bulls, 25 cows, ,,   39 elk.
    (This year bulls were not allowed to be
               shot in three drives.)
    1930 :   24 bulls, 14 cows, total 38 elk.

Another great day's shooting over this same ground occurred in September, 1888, details of which are given in the Badminton Library (Big Game Shooting: 1894: Vol. II: p. 136). The number of rifles is, unfortunately, not stated, but the day's sport was made up of three drives, the results of which were as follows : —

    1st Drive ... 24 elk.
    2nd ,,   ... 28 elk (bulls only).
    3rd ,,   ... 14 elk.
                    ———
    Total ... 66 elk.

Driving on a vast scale has been practised in Sweden for very many years, and on such great occasions as those mentioned above, several hundred beaters would form an immense cordon which would never be relaxed night or day. An enormous area of forest would thus be covered, the elk being moved gradually towards the positions where the guns were stationed.

Some splendid elk heads have been obtained in Sweden and their average size is rather larger than Norwegian heads.

In the great forest of Bialovieja, the Imperial preserve of the Emperor of Russia, great bags of elk and other game were made on the occasions of his annual shoot. I have already given in another chapter the details of the bag for 1900, made between the 31st August and 12th September, but I again give it in full owing to its great magnitude and variety. The total head of game killed is as follows*: —

Elk	36
Bison	42
Red Deer (Stags)	53
Deer (? Hinds)	26
Roe-deer (Bucks)	325
,, (Does)	3
Wild Boar	138
Foxes	51
Winged Game	11
Total	685

* Jean Stolzmann : *In litt*. 12th December 1900.

The Polish and Lithuanian elk heads are better than those from Norway.   One shot by Count Constantin Potocki in the Pinsk Marshes has a span of over 52 inches and a still finer one was formerly in the possession of the Czar.   Another great head was shot during the War in this same locality, where elk still exist in fair numbers.

In Norway, driving on a large scale never seems to have been attempted, tracking with the leash-dog or "bind-hund" being the usual method employed, though L. Lloyd in "Field Sports of the North of Europe" mentions an early record of elk being shot with the aid of pointers.   His statement is as follows: "Mr. Grieff speaks of killing the elk to pointers: he says, that about the year 1790, when he was residing in Westmanland, where those animals were at that time very numerous, he shot no fewer than eleven in the course of one season, to a favourite dog of his, called Caresse".

Few, if any, non-resident sportsmen had a more extensive knowledge of sport in Scandinavia than Sir Henry Pottinger, and in his interesting book "Flood, Fell and Forest", published in 1905, he states that in his best season he shot 8 bull elk and 1 cow.   Mr. H. J. Elwes shot 7 bull elk in twenty days' hunting in September, 1895, in the district of Mo, in the North Trondhjem

ELK

amt,[*] and in 1899 in Upper Namdalen, Mr. J. G. Millais shot 5 bull elk and a large bear during the course of a three weeks' hunt.[†]

Another very successful hunter in Norway is Mr. G. J. van Heek, Jr., of Enschede, Holland, who has kindly supplied me with some information concerning the best heads he has shot.[‡] On 12th September, 1913, at Slipern, Trondhjem Peninsular, he shot two bulls with horns having the following dimensions:—

	No. I.	No. II.
Greatest spread	48¾ ins.	33⅞ ins.
Breadth of palm ...	8¼ ins.	4¼ ins.
Circumference of burr ...	10⅝ ins.	7¼ ins.
Circumference of beam ...	6¾ ins.	5⅛ ins.
(Measured two inches above base of burr.)		
Points	10+9	5+5

In September, 1922, at Rocknedalen, Snaassen, he obtained two other first-class trophies, the dimensions of which I am able to give. No. I was shot on the 22nd September, and No. II on the 16th September.

[*] H. J. Elwes : "Memoirs of Travel, Sport, and Natural History" : 1930 : p. 155.
[†] Supplement to " Country Life " : 30th July 1910.
[‡] In litt. 22nd July 1931.

	No. I.	No. II.
Greatest spread	40½ ins.	40 ins.
Breadth of palm ...	4¾ ins.	7⅞ ins.
Circumference of burr ...	10¼ ins.	9 ins.
Circumference of beam ...	6¾ ins.	6¼ ins.
(Measured two inches above base of burr.)		
Points	5+6	6+7

Mr. van Heek has also hunted moose in Canada with notable success. On 6th October, 1925, he obtained a magnificent head in New-Brunswick with a spread of 61½ inches—an exceptional measurement for that country.

CHAPTER XVI

OTHER EUROPEAN GAME ANIMALS

REINDEER

WILD reindeer are to be found nearly as far north as the extreme limits of land, while they extend from Scandinavia in the west to Eastern Siberia, but their pursuit as a separate sport is practically confined to certain areas among the high fjelds of Norway, with a mean elevation of some 4,000 feet. The number of wild reindeer in Norway has fluctuated greatly from time to time, but the introduction of cheap magazine rifles and the facility with which they could be procured by the native hunters was the biggest factor in the reduction of their numbers. Legislation did something to restore the herds, but poaching in those desolate regions has usually been prevalent.

Stalking is practically the only accepted method of hunting these animals, though E. Demidoff (Prince San Donato) mentions shooting one at a drive in Central Ural.

219

Mr. Abel Chapman has given us some excellent descriptions of reindeer stalking at its best, in his fine, though now scarce, book ' Wild Norway ".

The largest bags of reindeer have I think been made by some of the native hunters and not by visiting sportsmen. There does not appear to be much reliable data concerning what the former actually achieved, but the Rev. M. R. Barnard in his book, "Sport in Norway", 1864, refers to this subject on page 97, and the details which were given to him, and which he quotes, are the largest bags I can find recorded. From this book I take the following : " B. tells me of a first-rate Vaage hunter who once killed 13 in a year, and he says that the great man of all, ' Old Joe ', who is I suppose, par excellence, the ' mighty hunter ' of Norway, who has been at it without cessation for fifty years, living almost all his life up in the high fjelds amongst the deer, has slain in his half-century between 500 and 600 ".

During Mr. Abel Chapman's last stalking season in Norway, a native hunter informed him that he had killed 33 deer the previous season and that he had commenced the present one with a bag of eleven out of one herd.*

Turning to the results of stalking, in which only really shootable beasts are killed, one of the most

* Abel Chapman : " Big Game Shooting " (The " Country Life " Library of Sport) : Vol. I : 1905 : p. 110.

successful hunts of more recent years was made by Captain P. B. Vanderbyl in 1907. This trip followed a five years' close season and reindeer were fairly numerous. Hunting from Lyseheien, Captain Vanderbyl shot eight stags, and F. C. Selous, who was his guest for part of the time, got five in seven days' hunting.*

IBEX

It seems certain that the European ibex would have ceased to exist in the Alps but for the intervention of King Victor Emanuel of Italy, in 1856. The superstitions of the middle-ages and later were responsible for the almost complete extermination of these animals. Their horns had a very considerable value, being made into goblets which were supposed to betray the presence of certain poisons, while various portions of the carcass were believed to possess healing powers for all manner of complaints; thus every mountaineer's hand was turned against them.

About 1821 the naturalist Zumstein prevailed upon the Piedmont Government to establish strict laws for the protection of the small band that existed in the Graian Alps, but this seems to have done little more than to delay the rate of decrease.

* J. G. Millais : " The Life of F. C. Selous " : 1918 : pp. 260/61.

In 1856, however, King Victor Emanuel created the preserve on both sides of the Dora Baltea which included their former reservation. The ibex thus became Royal game, and a staff of fifty-five keepers kept watch and ward over their numbers to such purpose that by 1877 they had increased to between 500 and 1,000 head, this in spite of the fact that the King shot on an average nearly fifty a year.

The Spanish ibex, which is a separate species, is perhaps the finest game beast to be found in Spain. Living among the highest peaks they afford splendid sport either by stalking or driving.

It is in the Royal preserves of the Dora Baltea in the Piedmont Alps that the largest bags of ibex have been made. Between 1856 and 1877 King Victor Emanuel was in the habit of visiting this retreat entirely alone, and it is said that the only sportsmen who were ever bidden by him to share the sport were Count Hoyos and Count Wilczek. The shooting was almost exclusively obtained by driving, and some 250 miles of bridle-paths are said to have been cut to enable the Royal sports-man to gain the elevated stands to which the beasts were driven. From 150 to 200 picked mountaineers circumvented the game and drove it to the well-known defiles where the rifle was stationed. Great skill was needed to successfully carry out these drives, the scene of the sport being at an altitude of from 6,000 to 12,000 feet and the beaters were often involved in extremely difficult climbs.

At the time of King Victor Emanuel's death his collection of horns, in his château-de-chasse, Sarre, near Aosta, totalled 232 pairs of male ibex horns, 22 pairs of female ibex horns, and over 700 pairs of chamois horns, and these figures probably represent the extent of his bag.

What the largest bag was as the result of a single day's shooting we do not definitely know, but according to Mr. W. A. Baillie-Grohman, the Rev. W. A. B. Coolidge has stated that he once saw 12 ibex and 25 chamois brought in as the spoils of one day's sport.*

King Humbert, who succeeded King Victor Emanuel, inherited a love for sport. He was a first-rate shot, his favourite weapon being a Holland and Holland .450 Express, and every year he repaired to the Alps for a fortnight's ibex and chamois shooting. The details of his bag are not available, but according to Count Scheibler he killed on an average fifty ibex a year.†

Ibex are also found in Greece, and in the Caucasus, where St. George Littledale shot seven

* " Sport in the Alps " : 1896 : p. 273.
† " Sport in Europe " : p. 216.

in the season of 1887. I have no exact information concerning the record bags for these countries, or for Spain, but I do not think they would approach the figures of the Piedmont Alps.

BEARS

The main haunts of the brown bear in Europe occur in Russia, Transylvania, Hungary and Scandinavia, though they are also met with locally in Roumania, Spain, and other parts. They attain their largest dimensions in Russia, where one shot by Count Andreas Potocki and stuffed in an erect attitude stands $7\frac{1}{2}$ feet high.

E. Demidoff (Prince San Donato) records a weight of 960 lbs. as being the heaviest within his knowledge from Eastern Siberia, and from European Russia he mentions one which weighed 800 lbs.

Bears may be killed by the ordinary methods of stalking or still hunting, by driving, by sitting up over a carcass in the spring, when the bears are eager for food, or, as is sometimes practised by the Lapps, by actually crawling into their snow-covered dens, one man in front with a rifle and another behind with a long pole at the end of which a lighted candle is fixed.

OTHER EUROPEAN GAME ANIMALS

In former times the bear had a much more extensive range in Europe than it has to-day, and it seems probable that the record bags were made in Saxony in the seventeenth century by those two great hunters, the Electors John George I and II. As the complete list of game killed by these Royal sportsmen has been given in Chapter XI, it is only necessary to state here that John George II is believed to have killed 239 bears, whilst the elder Elector killed only one less, though as has already been pointed out there is some doubt whether the 238 bears credited to the father includes those killed by the whole court personage, as the list in his own game diaries seems to show that he only killed 102 bears with his own hands.

With regard to individual bags of more recent times, "Snowfly" writing in "The Field" of June 2nd, 1906, says: "Hofjägmästare Falk, Lloyd, and the Finnish officer, Major Berndt Höök (who died within the three last years) have probably accounted individually for more bears in Northern Europe than any other sportsman of late years. The two first-named shot about 100 apiece to their own rifles, and the last, who did most of his hunting in the wilds of Russian Karelia, at least as many, besides being present at the death of quite double that number".

BIG GAME SHOOTING RECORDS

Falk and Lloyd shot most, if not all their bears in Scandinavia, and another celebrated hunter in that country was the Swede, Jan Svensson, who had twice been wounded by bears. Lloyd met him when he was between fifty and sixty years of age and he had then been concerned with the death of sixty or seventy of these animals, very many of which he had killed himself.*

It is probable that the record bag of bears obtained by driving was made in Sweden, where drives, or "skalls" on an enormous scale have been practised. "Snowfly," whom I have already quoted, writes as follows: " The greatest of these drives ever undertaken was carried out on June 25th, 26th and 27th, 1856. It took place at the northern end of the great Dalecarlin Lake Siljan, in the extensive forests along the Vanan, a tributary of the Vester Dal River; 4,000 men from the parishes of Mera, Sollerö, Elfdal, and Venjan formed the driving line, which, with the wings, extended over a distance of sixty kilometres. " On the two nights which intervened halts were made and huge fires were lit in order to prevent the wild animals from breaking back, and not until late on the third day was the place reached where the rifles were stationed.   Twenty-three

* I. Lloyd : " Field Sports of the North ".

226

bears, nine elk, three wolves, and a lynx were killed, a result which was considered highly satisfactory."

Géza Count Széchényi in a contribution to "Sport in Europe", 1901, p. 51, states that "a record bag was obtained by a party in Transylvania, ten or twelve guns bagging, if I remember right, twenty-eight bears in the course of three weeks, and in the same season another party shot twenty-two".

In the Kouban game preserves of the Grand Duke Serge of Russia, bears were regarded as vermin and his hunters are said to have shot on an average about eighty a year.*

* B. Demidoff (Prince San Donato) : "Sport in Europe : 1901 : p. 393.

CHAPTER XVII

AMERICAN BISON

THE bison of North America, often misnamed the buffalo in its native country, is not quite so tall as the European species, but owing to the thick frontlet and beard, and the shaggy coat of hair upon the neck and shoulders, which terminates at the knees in a mass of luxuriant locks, it has the appearance of being a bigger animal than is actually the case.

According to Mr. Hornaday, the range of the American bison formally extended over about one-third of North America. From the Atlantic coast it extended westward through a great tract of forest, across the Alleghany Mountains to the prairies of the Mississippi system, and across the Rocky Mountains into New Mexico, Utah, and Idaho. In its southern extension it reached the burning plains of North Eastern Mexico and northward it spread to the shores of the Great Slave Lake.

As an animal of the chase the American bison cannot be said to have ever afforded sport of a high order, their natural stupidity and indifference to man made them mere targets for riflemen rather than quarry which called for the arts of hunting. Of the various methods employed in their destruction, stalking, riding down, surrounding, hunting in snow-shoes, and shooting them at their drinking places, all proved effective, so effective, in fact, that in a few short years the vast herds which had roamed the prairies and forests for countless centuries were reduced almost to the point of extinction.

The greatest slaughter of the American bison occurred during the years 1872-3-4 and various estimates have been put forward concerning the number killed during that period. According to the Smithsonian reports, 1,491,000 bison were killed by white hunters in 1872 alone, and in the following year the number was exceeded by about 20,000 head.* These figures may be regarded as the most accurate computation made and they tally very closely with the carefully worked out estimate of Richard Irving Dodge, who arrived at the conclusion that 5,373,730 bison were killed by white men and Indians during these three years† According to Theodore Roosevelt it was about fifteen years from the time the destruction fairly began till the vast herds

* " The Field " : 25th August 1894.
† " The Hunting Grounds of the Great West " : 1877.

were exterminated, and by 1884 not a single herd of a hundred individuals existed.* Concerning the almost incredible numbers that formerly existed, two brief quotations will suffice. Theodore Roosevelt has described the experience of his friend Gen. W. H. Walker, of Virginia, on the upper Arkansas River in the early '50's, as follows: " He was camped with a scouting party on the banks of the river, and had gone out to try to shoot some meat. There were many buffaloes† in sight, scattered, according to their custom, in large bands. When he was a mile or two away from the river a dull roaring sound in the distance attracted his attention, and he saw that a herd of buffalo far to the south, away from the river, had been stampeded and was running his way. He knew that if he was caught in the open by the stampeded herd his chances of life would be small, and at once ran for the river. By desperate efforts he reached the breaks in the sheer banks just as the buffaloes reached them, and got into a position of safety on the pinnacle of a little bluff. From this point of vantage he could see the entire plain. To the very verge of the horizon the brown masses of the buffalo bands showed through the dust clouds, coming on with a thunderous roar like that of surf.

* " The Wilderness Hunter ": 1893 : p. 231.
† Bison.

Camp was a mile away, and the stampede luckily passed to one side of it. Watching his chance he finally dodged back to the tent, and all that afternoon watched the immense masses of buffalo, as band after band tore to the brink of the bluffs on one side, raced down them, rushed through the water, up the bluffs on the other side, and again off over the plain, churning the sandy, shallow stream into a ceaseless tumult. When darkness fell there was no apparent decrease in the numbers that were passing, and all through that night the continuous roar showed that the herds were still threshing across the river. Towards dawn the sound at last ceased, and General Walker arose somewhat irritated, as he had reckoned on killing an ample supply of meat, and he supposed that there would be now no bison left south of the river. To his astonishment, when he strolled up on the bluffs and looked over the plain, it was still covered far and wide with groups of buffalo, grazing quietly. Apparently there were as many on that side as ever, in spite of the many scores of thousands that must have crossed over the river during the stampede of the afternoon and night ".

Mr. William Blackmore in his Introduction to " The Hunting Grounds of the Great West " writes: " In the autumn of 1868, whilst crossing the Plains on the Kansas Pacific Railroad—for a distance of upwards of 120 miles, between Ellsworth and Sheridan, we passed through an almost unbroken herd of buffalo. The Plains were blackened with them, and more than once the train had to stop to allow unusually large herds to pass. A few years afterwards, when travelling over the same line of railroad, it was a rare sight to see a few herds of from ten to twenty buffalo ".

Frank Carver is said to have killed 5,500 bison in his best year, and in eighteen months as buffalo hunter for the construction crew of the Kansas Pacific Railway, Cody (Buffalo Bill) killed 4,280.* An old-time buffalo hunter informed Mr. Clive Phillips-Wolley that he himself had accounted for 3,500 head in four years and that a friend of his, A. C. Myers, once killed 4,200 buffaloes in the Pan Handle Country, in Texas, in one year, about the time Hayes was President.†

Colonel Dodge states that he once counted 112 carcasses inside of a semi-circle of 200 yards radius, all of which were killed by one man from the same spot, and in less than three-quarters of an hour,‡ whilst in 1873, on the Canadian River,

* E. Douglas Branch : " The Hunting of the Buffalo " : 1929 : pp. 200 and 142.
† Badminton Library : " Big Game Shooting " : 1894 : Vol. I : p. 380.
‡ " The Hunting Grounds of the Great West " : 1877 : p. 136.

Charlie Rath is said to have shot 107 bison at one stand.* This methodical butchery was made possible owing to the fact that so long as the hunter remained concealed he could often shoot beast after beast with well-directed shots, whilst the dwindling band of survivors, instead of running away, would gather in astonishment around their dead or dying comrades. Armed usually with the accurate " Sharp " rifle, weighing about 16 lbs., and with other men to do the skinning, and a spare man to look after camp and do odd jobs, the actual shooter had practically nothing else to do but shoot, and many became wonderfully proficient in their ghastly trade. Hunting on horseback was doubtless a somewhat more exciting form of killing them. A good horse ridden by a man who understood his business could overtake a herd before they had gone 200 yards, and then, if so minded, the hunter could ride clean through it, splitting it in two and thereby being more easily enabled to select his victims. The possibilities of this form of hunting are well exemplified by Col. Dodge who says: " Once when on a hunt I came upon two Mexican buffalo hunters, one of whom possessed the finest and most perfectly trained buffalo horse I have

* E. Douglas Branch : " The Hunting of the Buffalo " : 1929 : p. 200.

ever seen. They were encamped near a water hole to which the buffalo came to drink. On the approach of a herd the horses were saddled, the fine horse and rider dashed into it, split it up . . . , singled out a victim, always a fat two-year-old, separated it entirely from its companions, and headed it towards camp, when a pistol shot finished the race. They had a fine lot of meat and a goodly pile of skins, and they said that every buffalo had been driven into camp and killed as the one I saw ". In this there is a touch of artistry, but what can be said of the methods adopted in the country south of the South Platte where the land was waterless for miles and the bison had to resort to the river as their only drinking place. As each herd approached the water it was met by bullets, and every effort was made to prevent the survivors from quenching their thirst. Again and again the unfortunate beasts would approach the water, and at every approach some of their number would be shot down, whilst at night time. fires were lighted and the shooting still kept up. In many places, says Col. Dodge, the valley was offensive from the stench of putrefying carcasses. So died the incalculable herds of the American bison—the greatest sacrifice of wild life to commercialism that the world has ever known.

AMERICAN BISON

With the advent of the white man they were bound to go sooner or later, and the market for their robes, tongues, and meat, merely hastened the day. It is easy for one generation to judge the actions of another, but it should be remembered that the " buffalo-hunters " were often men, who, for better or for worse, had taken their chance in a new country with all the hardships that that connotes. If they were disappointed in their digging for gold, or in their thousand and one other ambitions, then they turned to the seemingly limitless crop of bison. The harvest was easily gathered and the slaughter was only stayed just in time to save this noble looking beast from total extermination.

CHAPTER XVIII

MOOSE

THESE splendid animals are the largest living representatives of the deer family, and in Alaska, where they attain their largest size, they may stand 6 ft. 9 in. at the shoulder. In that country they are acknowledged to be a separate race and are known as *Alces gigas*, as distinct from *Alces americanus*, which occur further south. Moose, in common with other North American animals, have been enormously reduced in numbers. According to Lockhart, who wrote in 1865, they were then common over practically the whole of British America, but their present range is said to be restricted mainly to Alaska, Montana, Nova Scotia, and New Brunswick. In the summer, moose are usually found in the neighbourhood of swamps, lakes, or rivers, but in winter they move to higher ground, and at all times they are lovers of dense forest.

Stalking or still-hunting is the form of hunting most commonly employed in their pursuit, but locally the practice of calling them with an artificial call is followed.

MOOSE

Formerly moose were slaughtered in their "yards" when imprisoned by the snows of winter, and a great many were also killed by fire-hunting, or hunting by torchlight, and by running them down on snow-shoes in deep snow.

Doubtless the record bag of moose, irrespective of age and sex, belongs to some meat hunter of the long ago, but I think the most noteworthy bag ever made by a sportsman stands to the credit of Mr. A. S. Reed, who, in a single hunting trip to Cooks Inlet, Alaska, at the beginning of the present century, obtained six heads, of which five had the following dimensions* : —

			Span.
No. I.	...	...	76 inches.
„ II.	...	...	72 „
„ III.	...	...	67 „
„ IV.	...	...	66 „
„ V.	...	...	65 „

Concerning this wonderfully successful trip Mr. Clive Phillips-Wolley has written as follows: "The six 'heads' killed by Mr. Reed in Cook's Inlet represent, I fancy, the most successful moose hunt ever made by a white man, and if you add to these six monsters nine bears, the largest of which measured over 10 feet in length, five

Clive Phillips-Wolley : " Big Game Shooting " (The " Country Life " Library of Sport) : 1905 : Vol. I : pp. 156-157-158.

cariboo, some white sheep (*O. dalli*), and walrus, it will be admitted, possibly, that no finer trophies of a single hunt have ever been brought out of the north.

" Both the bears and the cariboo were honoured with new scientific names, and no heads were shot which were not exceptional."

Mr. Reed's best moose head, if judged by points and breadth of palm, is still, I think, one of the finest, if not the finest head in the world. I believe he once shot an even larger one with a span of over 80 inches, but this was completely destroyed by fire together with the cabin against which the head was leaning.

Mr. Reed is said to have seen ninety moose during one " fall " in Alaska, and he undoubtedly obtained the finest collection of big game trophies from that country that have ever fallen to the rifle of a sportsman.

Since his wonderfully successful expeditions, Major C. R. E. Radclyffe, accompanied by Mr. R. F. Glyn, visited Alaska in 1903, when they obtained 6 moose in a representative bag of the big game of the country.* In three trips to various parts of North America between the years 1900 and 1906, F. C. Selous shot 6 moose, among

* Major C. R. E. Radclyffe · " Big Game Shooting in Alaska " : 1904 · p 73.

238

them being one very massive head of 67 inches which he obtained in September, 1904, on the north fork of the Macmillan River in the Yukon. Lord Elphinstone, Paul Niedieck and many other well-known sportsmen have achieved notable successes, but for quality and quantity combined Mr. Reed's achievements with moose seem to stand alone.

A notable performance in connection with moose hunting has been recorded by Theodore Roosevelt, who says*: "One of the most successful moose-hunters I know is Colonel Cecil Clay of the Department of Law in Washington; he it was who killed the moose composing the fine group mounted by Mr. Hornaday in the National Museum. Colonel Clay lost his right arm in the Civil War, but is an expert rifle-shot nevertheless, using a short, light 44-calibre old-style Winchester carbine. With this weapon he has killed over a score of moose, by fair still-hunting ".

† " Hunting Adventures in the West " (The Wilderness Hunter) 1927 : p. 174.

CHAPTER XIX

WAPITI

THE North American wapiti, commonly called the elk, or round-horned elk in its native country, is certainly one of the grandest members of the deer tribe. A really first-class wapiti head is one of the finest trophies of the chase, but great heads such as were obtained in the middle of the last century are seldom if ever met with now. In this connection it is interesting to note that the wapiti imported into New Zealand give promise of producing heads equal to the best from North America. According to W. A. Perry, the wapiti was formerly found in nearly all parts of the United States, in Mexico, and in British America as far as the 60th parallel of north latitude, but it is now restricted to eastern North America.

Wapiti are more easily approached than red deer, but since they have retreated before civilisation and are now more frequently found in dense timber country, their pursuit is far more arduous than was formerly the case. In former times bands of a thousand and more individuals were to be seen in open country, but those days have gone for ever, and the hunter of to-day can no longer pick and choose his heads from the vast throngs that once roamed the Continent.

Though the destruction of wapiti in North America never assumed the proportions of the organized slaughter of the bison, they suffered but little less. Slowly but surely the great bands dwindled and dwindled before the incessant persecution of the hide-hunters, meat-hunters and others. Mr. W. A. Baillie-Grohman mentions a terrible example of wanton destruction. He writes as follows*: " In severe winters Nature seemed occasionally to assist the work of extermination. Thus, in a severe blizzard which swept over Colorado in the last week of January, 1893, a band of about 1,000 wapiti became imprisoned by the snow on a high and heavily timbered mesa in the mountains near Steamboat Springs. Ranchmen, prospectors, and hide hunters, on hearing of this windfall, ' waded in,' killing many with clubs, as the local papers reported, and I believe not a single beast was allowed to escape ".

Turning to legitimate big game hunters, the finest bag of wapiti bulls that I can find recorded was made by Mr. Andrew Williamson in the

* " Fifteen Years' Sport and Life in the Hunting Grounds of Western America and British Columbia " : 1900 : p. 33.

season of 1879 in Colorado. The 16 heads that he obtained during this trip averaged as follows[*] : —

> Length of antlers . 53 inches.
> Span . . . 44 „
> Girth above burr . 10¼ „

The following are the summarized particulars of eight of Mr. Williamson's bulls : —

Measurements of eight of the sixteen bull wapiti shot by Mr. Andrew Williamson in Colorado in 1879.

	1	2	3	4	5	6	7	8
Length of Antlers	49"	56"	54"	54"	52"	53"	49½"	49"
	+	+	+	.	+	+	+	+
	59½"	59"	54½"	55½"	55"	51"	51"	50"
Span .	50"	51"	42"	45"	51"	42"	47½"	43"
Girth above burr	10½"	12½"	11½"	10½"	10½"	—	10"	—
Points . .	11	16	14	14	16	13	12	13
Height at withers	16 hds 1½"	16 hds	16½ hds	16 hds. 1"	16 hds	—	15 hds 3"	16 hds. ½"
Length from tail to nose .	8' 7"	8' 4"	8' 6"	8' 6"	8' 2"	—	8' 0"	8' 5"
Girth round heart	6' 2"	6' 1"	6' 4"	6' 0"	5' 10"	—	5' 11"	5' 10"

In 1880, Mr. Williamson published an account of his trip in a book entitled " Sport and Photography in the Rocky Mountains ". Though this work contains little more than fifty pages it gives an excellent account of his experiences, and it is a most beautiful production. Mr. Williamson was an expert photographer, and though the

* Andrew Williamson : " Sport and Photography in the Rocky Mountains " : 1880 : p. 38.

242

WAPITI

photographs were taken so many years ago they are of quite exceptional excellence.

Referring to the results of his expedition, he says: " My bag of big game comprised but thirty-two head, all told. I could with ease, had I desired it, have more than trebled the number. . . . . During the whole trip I never shot a stag whose head I did not bring home as a trophy; never fired at a hind; that we only killed such blacktail as we really needed, and that, save in the case of the grizzly bear, we never lost a wounded animal ".

Unfortunately, very few men who hunted in North America in the seventies and eighties of last century have left such exact statistics of their sport. During that period in Wyoming, Mr. Frank Cooper killed two heads of 63¾ inches and 62¼ inches, and in the same country, Sir H. Seton-Karr shot two of 61 inches and 59½ inches. On the borders of Wyoming and Idaho, Mr. W. A. Baillie-Grohman killed a 64-inch head, but unfortunately it was destroyed when the log cabin in which it was stored was burnt to the ground. The same sportsman also obtained two other heads, both in Wyoming, of 60¾ inches and 60¼ inches. Full details of the bags made by these men are not known, but in their time Wyoming was one of the finest game countries in the world, and it is possible that W. A. Baillie-Grohman, who spent fifteen years in Western America, obtained the greatest number of really first-class wapiti heads that have ever been shot by one man. In addition to those heads that he kept himself he enriched more than one Continental collection with splendid trophies.

In 1877, in Wyoming, H. Seton-Karr and Thomas Bate obtained between them some thirty good wapiti heads as well as examples of antelope, blacktail deer, and bison, also a grizzly and a big-horn ram. An excellent account of this trip is to be found in "My Sporting Holidays", by Sir Henry Seton-Karr, which was published in 1904.

CHAPTER XX

NORTH AMERICAN BEARS

THERE are several kinds of bears to be found in North America, but just how many distinct varieties exist would be more difficult to say. Some naturalists have been inclined to name varieties on the strength of differences which may well be nothing more than local variations. Many of the old hunters were also at variance on this subject, some holding the view that the so-called silver-tips, cinnamon bears, roach-backs, etc., were distinct varieties, whilst others called them all grizzlies. In the following pages I refer to the black bear, to the grizzly (or to bears of that type), and to the still larger animals that are found in Alaska. With the polar bear we are not concerned. The black bear is the commonest and most widely distributed of them all. It is also the smallest and is not usually a very formidable opponent. The grizzly bear is an animal of quite three times the size, and under certain circumstances it is a decidedly dangerous beast. President Roosevelt has stated that he has personally known of eight cases in which men have met their deaths by following grizzlies into

thick cover. The Alaskan bears, particularly
those found on the Peninsular, are still larger
animals. Bears have been hunted in all manner
of ways. In the southern States, black bears
have been followed with horse and hound and
shot with the rifle or shot-gun, and they have also
been killed with no other weapon than the knife.
In open country grizzlies have been ridden and
shot with revolvers, and they have sometimes
been roped by cowboys. All varieties are more
commonly killed by stalking or still-hunting, and
they are also taken in traps, though the last-
named method does not come within the scope of
this book.

General Wade Hampton is said to have been
in at the death of 500 bears, most of which, if
not all, were of the black variety. Of this vast
total, at least two-thirds are said to have fallen
by his own hand. He once killed 68 bears in
five months in Mississippi, and on one occasion
he killed 4 bears in a day.*

Concerning this great hunter, President
Roosevelt writes as follows: "General Wade
Hampton, who has probably killed more black
bears than any other man living in the United
States, frequently used the knife, slaying thirty
or forty with this weapon. His plan was, when

* Theodore Roosevelt : " The Wilderness Hunter " : 1893 : p. 259.

he found that the dogs had a bear at bay, to walk up close and cheer them on. They would instantly seize the bear in a body, and he would then rush in and stab it behind the shoulder, reaching over so as to inflict the wound on the opposite side from that where he stood. He escaped scathless from all these encounters save one, in which he was rather severely torn in the forearm. . . . . General Hampton always hunted with large packs of hounds, managed sometimes by himself and sometimes by his negro hunters. He occasionally took out forty dogs at a time. He found that all his dogs together could not kill a big fat bear, but they occasionally killed three-year-olds, or lean and poor bears. . . . . The two largest bears he himself killed weighed, respectively, 408 and 410 lbs. They were both shot in Mississippi. But he saw at least one bear killed which was much larger than either of these. These figures were taken down at the time, when the animals were actually weighed on the scales. Most of his hunting for bear was done in northern Mississippi, where one of his plantations was situated, near Greenville ".

R. I. Dodge once shot 5 black bears in a single day, his own description of this feat being as follows*: " It is difficult to find him (the black

---

* " Hunting Grounds of the Great West " : 1877 : pp. 216/217.

bear) without dogs, though in the berry season, many years ago, I bagged without a dog no less than five in one day, catching them in little patches of plum or hackberry bushes, dashing up on horseback and shooting them with a revolver as they ran ".

With regard to the grizzly bear, the largest bag I can find mentioned was made by one known as Old Ike, who is said to have shot nearly a hundred bears. It is not quite clear whether all these were grizzly bears, but Theodore Roosevelt refers to him in " The Wilderness Hunter " in a chapter devoted to hunting the grizzly.* He says: " One of the most successful bear hunters I ever knew, an old fellow whose real name I never heard as he was always called Old Ike, was killed . . . . in the spring or early summer of 1886 on one of the head-waters of the Salmon. He was a very good shot, had killed nearly a hundred bears with the rifle, and, although often charged, had never met with any accident, so that he had grown somewhat careless. On the day in question he had met a couple of mining prospectors and was travelling with them, when a grizzly crossed his path. The old hunter imme- diately ran after it, rapidly gaining, as the bear did not hurry when it saw itself pursued, but

* " Hunting Grounds of the Great West " : 1877 : p. 317.

slouched slowly forwards, occasionally turning its head to grin and growl. It soon went into a dense grove of young spruce, and as the hunter reached the edge it charged fiercely out. He fired one hasty shot, evidently wounding the animal, but not seriously enough to stop or cripple it; and as his two companions ran forward they saw the bear seize him with its wide-spread jaws, forcing him to the ground. They shouted and fired, and the beast abandoned the fallen man on the instant and sullenly retreated into the spruce thicket, whither they dared not follow it. Their friend was at his last gasp; for the whole side of the chest had been crushed in by one bite, the lungs showing between the rent ribs ".

An extraordinary feat of hunting in connection with the grizzly bear was once performed by General Jackson. It was some years before the Civil War and Jackson was then a young officer in the Mounted Rifle Regiment. Describing this incident, President Roosevelt says : " While on a scout after hostile Indians, the troops in their march roused a large grizzly which sped off across the plain in front of them. Strict orders had been issued against firing at game, because of the nearness of the Indians. Young Jackson was a man of great strength, a keen swordsman, who always kept the finest edge on his blade, and he was on a swift and mettled Kentucky horse, which luckily had but one eye. Riding at full speed he soon overtook the quarry. As the horse hoofs sounded nearer, the grim bear ceased its flight, and whirling round stood at bay, raising itself on its hind-legs and threatening its pursuer with bared fangs and spread claws. Carefully riding his horse so that its blind side should be towards the monster, the cavalryman swept by at a run, handling his steed with such daring skill that he just cleared the blow of the dreaded fore-paw, while with one mighty sabre stroke he cleft the bear's skull, slaying the grinning beast as it stood upright ".

Mr. W. T. Hornaday states that " Mr. W. H. Wright, a very successful bear-hunter, once killed seven bears in one day* ", though whether they were all grizzly bears is not quite clear.

With regard to the great bears that are found in Alaska, Mr. A. S. Reed shot 9 of these animals in a single season at the beginning of the present century. I have already given particulars of this wonderful hunting trip in the chapter devoted to Moose, so it is unnecessary to repeat the details in full, though it may be mentioned that in addition to these 9 bears, Mr. Reed shot 6 moose, 5 caribou, some white sheep, and walrus.

* " Camp-Fires in the Canadian Rockies " : 1906 : p. 176.

NORTH AMERICAN BEARS

In 1903, Major C. R. E. Radclyffe and Mr. R. F. Glyn, accompanied by Mr. Clifford Little, who acted as hunter and taxidermist, undertook an expedition to Alaska. On the Alaska Peninsular, where the bears are probably the largest in Alaska, the party accounted for 12, and in all they bagged 15 bears.* Major Radclyffe's largest bear measured from nose to tail in a straight line was 7 feet 5 inches. The following is the total list of game bagged, including a few odd caribou or sheep which the natives killed for meat† : —

Brown Bears	13
Black Bears	2
Moose	6
Sheep	15
Caribou	7
Seal	3
Fox	2
Otter	1
Wolverine	1
Porcupine	6
Rabbits	31
Eagles	3
Grouse and Ptarmigan . . .	108

Geese, ducks, and various varieties
   of other birds, in all about 60 species.

* Major C. R. E. Radclyffe : " Big Game Shooting in Alaska " 1904 : pp. 48 and 73.
† ibid. p. 73.

CHAPTER XXI

OTHER NORTH AMERICAN GAME ANIMALS

IF it were possible to ascertain the actual facts, it would probably be found that all the largest bags of North American animals were made by the pioneer settlers, who, if they were not conducting ferocious warfare against the Indians, were playing havoc with the vast herds of game that then inhabited the Continent. Such men as Daniel Boone and his fellow hunters formed the spear-head of the vast armies that so quickly conquered the wilderness. No finer pen-picture of those early hunters has ever been made than that written by that great sportsman and President of the U.S.A., Theodore Roosevelt—from his excellent book, " The Wilderness Hunter ". I take the following extracts : " Where they pitched their camps and built their log huts or stockaded hamlets, towns grew up, and men who were tillers of the soil, not mere wilderness wanderers, thronged in to take and hold the land. Then, ill-at-ease among the settlements for which they had themselves made ready the way, and fretted even by the slight restraints of the rude and un- couth semi-civilization of the border, the restless hunters moved onward into the yet unbroken wilds where the game dwelt and the red tribes marched for ever to war and hunting. Their untamable souls ever found something congenial and beyond measure attractive in the lawless freedom of the lives of the very savages against whom they warred so bitterly. . . . .

" Very characteristic in its way was the career of quaint, honest, fearless Davy Crockett, the Tennessee rifleman and Whig Congressman, per- haps the best shot in all our country, whose skill in the use of his favourite weapon passed into a proverb, and who ended his days by a hero's death in the ruins of the Alamo. An even more notable man was another mighty hunter, Houston, who when a boy ran away to the Indians; who while still a lad returned to his own people to serve under Andrew Jackson in the campaigns which the greatest of all the back- woods' leaders waged against the Creeks, the Spaniards, and the British. He was wounded at the storming of one of the strongholds of Red Eagle's doomed warriors, and returned to his

Tennessee home to rise to high civil honor, and
become the foremost man of his State.   Then,
while Governor of Tennessee, in a sudden fit of
moody anger, and of mad longing for the un-
fettered life of the wilderness, he abandoned his
office, his people, and his race, and fled to the
Cherokees beyond the Mississippi. For years he
lived as one of their chiefs; until one day, as he
lay in ignoble ease and sloth, a rider from the
south, from the rolling plains of the San Antonio
and Brazos, brought word that the Texans were
up, and in doubtful struggle striving to wrest
their freedom from the lancers and carabineers of
Santa Anna.   Then his dark soul flamed again
into burning life; riding by night and day he
joined the risen Texans, was hailed by them as a
heaven-sent leader, and at the San Jacinto led
them on to the overthrow of the Mexican host.
Thus the stark hunter, who had been alternately
Indian fighter and Indian chief, became the
President of the New Republic, and, after its
admission into the United States, a Senator at
Washington; and, to his high honor, he remained to the end of his days staunchly loyal to
the flag of the Union."

Game-books and shooting diaries were things
unknown to men of this type, so that for our
" record bags " we have to search elsewhere.

OTHER N. AMERICAN GAME ANIMALS

CARIBOU

The reindeer of Northern Europe and the caribou of North America, inclusive of its local phases, forms a genus by itself which is distinguished from other deer by the form of the antlers and their presence in both sexes. Zoologists are inclined to subdivide the caribou into many local races, some of which can be regarded as varieties of the woodland caribou, and others as varieties of the barren-ground caribou. From the point of view of the hunter they are all much the same animal, and for the purpose of these notes I do not differentiate between them. All caribou are subject to migration to a greater or less extent. In the autumn of 1889, Warburton Pike witnessed the mighty migration south of the barren-ground caribou. Ptarmigan in thousands, wolves, wolverines, and arctic foxes, together with some scattered bands of caribou, preceded the main masses which took no less than six days to pass Pike's encampment.

The horns of caribou are subject to infinite variation, animals in the same herd sometimes having horns of quite different types. They are inquisitive creatures and not very keen-sighted.

Though caribou have been killed in various ways, stalking is probably the only method which concerns the big game hunter, and their pursuit does not present any exceptional difficulties to an experienced hunter.

According to that great authority, Mr. Warburton Pike, it is quite a common occurrence for a band of Indians to kill several hundred barren-ground caribou at a time, by spearing them from canoes after they have been driven into a lake, but it would be quite impossible, even if it were desirable, to obtain accurate records of this nature. Vast numbers have also been shot on migration, but these wholesale killings do not come within the province of legitimate big game hunting.

So far as I know, the man who obtained the finest collection of first-class caribou heads was Mr. J. G. Millais. Mr. Millais spent four seasons in Newfoundland, hunting and mapping parts of the interior, and during this time he shot 52 male and 4 female caribou.* Among them were heads with 49, 45, 44, 40. and 35 points, and four of these were magnificent specimens. The following are the dimensions taken from his beautiful book, " Newfoundland and its Untrodden Ways ", of the first three of these heads : —

* J. G. Millais : "The Gun at Home and Abroad" : 1915 : Vol. IV : p. 273.

No. I. 49 *pointer shot on the Upper Gander,
near Little Gull, in* 1903.

    Length on outer curve . . 36 inches.

    Circumference above bay . 7 „

    Widest inside . . . 29 „

A perfect Newfoundland head in every respect.

No. II. 45 *pointer shot near Tamnapegawi Lake
in* 1906.

    Length on outer curve . 46½ inches.

    Circumference above bay . 5½ „

    Widest inside . . . 31 „

One of, if not the finest Newfoundland head
known.

No. III. 44 *pointer shot on the Upper Gander
in* 1903.

    Length on outer curve . . 42 inches.

    Circumference above bay . 6 „

    Widest inside . . . 34 „

A very fine head with heavy tops and large
brows, the bays form its only weakness.

Mr. Millais also obtained two notable heads in
Cassiar. The first, though of no great length, it
is only 40 inches, has 53 good points.* " The
beautiful symmetry of the head is attained by the
length and ' wildness ' of the long snags of the
upper branches, some of which are 17½ inches

* " Country Life " : 23rd October 1909.

long, forming in places a double row." This splendid beast was bagged out of a herd that contained many fine heads. Mr. Millais writes as follows: "Over fifty caribou lay in one herd, and among them were twelve huge bulls, the smallest carrying a head any hunter would have been proud to possess. I looked them over with greedy anticipation. Some had great long horns, one about 58 inches or 60; another had splendid tops but poor brows; another had a very beautiful, spindly head, broken up at the top in two bifurcating beams, each with long, irregular points; but the king of them all was the biggest stag which lay at the top and carried the finest pointy head I had ever seen". His second notable head from Cassiar was 56 inches in length. The principal feature of this head is the enormous development of the tops.

I must here mention that I had hoped to obtain certain first-hand information from Mr. J. G. Millais, and indeed, in the early stages of writing this book, he did supply me with valuable advice and assistance, but before I had proceeded far it was with the deepest regret that I learnt of his death. A first-rate shot with both rifle and gun, a good fisherman, and a capable artist, he also had a most extensive knowledge of horticulture and arboriculture. At one time and another he filled with distinction the rôles of soldier, sailor, and British Consul, but he will probably be remembered best as a field naturalist and the author of many splendid books on natural history and sport.   In this capacity he was second to none, and during his lifetime he accomplished an enormous amount of work.   He possessed the rare gift of being able to transmit to others, by pencil, brush, and word, the charm and beauty of nature which fascinated him so deeply from the cradle to the grave.   If his passing leaves a blank in many circles, his works remain as a monument to a noble and purposeful life.

MULE-DEER

Mule-deer, so called on account of the enormous size of their ears, are somewhat lacking in grace compared with certain members of the deer tribe.   They are stoutly built animals, and their horns, which are of a complex character, are subject to variations from the normal type.   A really good mule-deer head makes quite a handsome trophy.   They are usually found in rough broken country and their pursuit thus demands the methods of the " still-hunter " rather than the " stalker " where the game is spied from a distance and then stalked to within range.   Mule-deer are infrequently referred to as black-tails, particularly by early writers on North American sport.

Some twenty-five miles or so from Fort Lyon, Richard Irving Dodge once shot 31 mule-deer in one week.* Concerning this week's shooting he writes as follows: " I once spent a week at a fine spring in the heart of a series of cānons, which more abounded in black-tails† than any locality I have ever seen. It was on this occasion that I bagged thirty-one. The constant presence of men, horses, and dogs had no effect to frighten away the deer, and one or more were bagged early each morning, sometimes within a few hundred yards of camp ".

WHITE-TAILED DEER

The white-tailed deer and its immediate relatives afford sport to a greater number of hunters than any other game animal in America. They may be pursued by hounds followed by mounted hunters armed with rifles, or by driving them to " stands " where the hunters are concealed, or by the ordinary methods of stalking or still-hunting. Like all North American deer they love well-

* R. I. Dodge : " Hunting Grounds of the Great West " : 1877 : pp. 181-182.
† Dodge in common with many hunters of his time refers to male-deer as black-tails.

timbered country, but their habits and appearance are too well known to call for any special comment.

The largest bag of these animals that I can find recorded was made by Richard Irving Dodge. Referring to a lovely valley in the Guadalupe Mountains he writes as follows[*]: " I obtained permission to go on a hunt, and arrived in that valley about noon one day, hunted that afternoon, all next, and until noon the third day. My bag to my own hand was five black bear and twenty-three deer, which altogether being as much as my pack mules could possibly carry, I was forced to return to my post before my hunt was half out. This was an exceptional oasis. The foot of white man had probably never before trod it. The Indians being debarred by superstition from entering it, the game for several years had been entirely undisturbed, and knew nothing of the danger of the presence of man ".

BLACK-TAILED DEER

The description " black-tailed deer " is sometimes used somewhat indiscriminately, but I refer here to the Columbian black-tailed deer. This species has a very restricted distribution as it is apparently confined to the mountain-ranges

[*] R. I. Dodge : " Hunting Grounds of the Great West " : 1877 : p. 191.

bordering the Pacific in the neighbourhood of the Columbia River and it is said to be unknown to the eastwards of the Sierra Nevada. In size it is rather smaller than the mule-deer and with relatively smaller ears. Its antlers are of the same type as the mule-deer's and very similar in appearance.

I do not know what is the largest bag of these animals obtained by fair hunting and by shooting bucks only, but Mr. Clive Phillips-Wolley has recorded that in 1893 two half-breeds (excellent shots and woodsmen) are reported to have killed 22 of these deer in a single day in the neighbourhood of Victoria.*

PRONGHORN ANTELOPE

The pronghorn antelope, or prongbuck, is the only representative of a family closely allied to the Bovidæ, though distinguished by the fact that the sheaths of the horns of the males are forked and shed annually. They are exceedingly swift, though their endurance is not great and they are unable to jump. They are shy and timid by nature though their curiosity will sometimes lead them to within easy range of the hunter. Prongbucks congregate in herds and frequent open

* Badminton Library : " Big Game Shooting " : 1894 : Vol. I : p. 423.

OTHER N. AMERICAN GAME ANIMALS

prairie country in the temperate regions of the western portion of North America, though their range was formerly more extensive than it is to-day. They may be hunted by the ordinary methods of stalking and they also afford good sport if coursed with powerful greyhounds.

The largest bag of antelope made by one man in a single season that I have found recorded was made by one Sam Wells, " who, when the Union Pacific Railway was being built to the west of Cheyenne, killed, in his capacity of meat-hunter to the construction party, 84 antelope, 24 elk (wapiti) and 18 deer during one autumn ".*

Richard Irving Dodge states that on one occasion he stalked a large herd feeding in an open glade, surrounded by rocks and cedar thickets. Unable to locate the sound of the rifle, or to see any dust, they rushed round and round the glade, and only escaped after he had knocked down seven of their number.†

It is probable that considerably larger bags have been made though I have been unable to obtain exact details. According to Sir Henry Seton-Karr " a bag of 20 or 30 antelope was not an uncommon morning's work for an old hand when the Union Pacific Railway was being laid".‡

* Clive Phillips-Wolley : Badminton Library : " Big Game Shooting " : 1894 : Vol I : p. 404.
† " Hunting Grounds of the Great West " : 1877 : p 199.
‡ " My Sporting Holidays " : 1904 : pp. 152/3.

CHAPTER XXII

SOME RECORDS OF ALL SORTS.

IN the course of my researches I came across the accounts of various feats performed with the rifle, and of incidents in connection with the pursuit of animals, which, though not coming strictly within the province of this work, seemed worthy of collection. I do not put them forward as records, but on account of their rareness, curiosity, or other interest.

Rabbits. cannot by any stretch of the imagination be regarded as big game, but they are sometimes shot with low-velocity, small-bore rifles. A remarkable bag of this nature was recorded in "The Field" of 11th September, 1877: In the course of a single afternoon's sport in Lincolnshire, Mr. H. W. L. Haigh shot 123 rabbits as they came out of their holes. The average range was about fifty yards and they were killed with a .250 rifle by Holland and Holland firing hollow bullets.

SOME RECORDS OF ALL SORTS

Another extraordinary piece of shooting with a " rook and rabbit rifle " was recorded in " The Field " of 10th October, 1931. Mr. Harry Clifton, writing from Kildalton Castle, Isle of Islay, stated that he had recently taken a guest, " Lord Dunsany, out for an hour before dinner, and he took a .250 rifle to pot a rabbit or two. This was the eventual bag: One woodcock, one snipe (shot on the wing), two blackcock and two rabbits ".

Shooting in India in 1883, Colonel Howard got 1 ravine deer (buck), 1 bustard, 2 peafowl, 1 sandgrouse, and 1 duck in a day, all shot with a rifle.[*]

On certain estates in the Highlands of Scotland, days which yield sport to rifle, rod, and gun are possible, and the feat of killing a stag, a grouse, and a salmon in a day, has, judging by the sporting press, been accomplished by a good many individuals. The most remarkable of these mixed days that I have found recorded was achieved by Lieut.-Col. C. Beddington, at Glendye, Kincardineshire, on October 13th, 1930. Starting at 6.30 a.m. with the idea of trying to get a stag, a salmon, a grouse, and a blackcock, he finished the

[*] Badminton Library : " Big Game Shooting " : 1894 : Vol. II : p. 352.

day at dusk with the following bag to his credit* :

- 2 Stags.
- 1 Roe-deer (killed with the rifle, running at over 200 yards).
- 6 Pheasants.
- 4 Blackgame.
- 4 Partridges.
- 2 Grouse.
- 1 Merganser.
- 1 Heron.
- 1 Rabbit.
- 2 Salmon (one killed on fly and one with worm).

Total 24 head.

Mr. W. Steuart Menzies, of Culdares, shooting and fishing at Glen Lyon on a day in September, 1918, obtained the following: In the morning, grouse, blackgame, snipe, golden plover, partridge, wild duck, woodcock; and in the afternoon, 1 stag, 1 roe, and 1 salmon weighing 28 lbs. Mr. Steuart Menzies was unaccompanied all day and he had to carry his salmon two and a half miles home, and row over the River Lyon.†

The shooting of three stags and a driven salmon (with the rifle) is certainly an unusual feat, but Mr. P. R. C(halmers) has described such a day, when

* " The Field " : 8th November 1930.
† ibid. 6th December 1930.

SOME RECORDS OF ALL SORTS

he, as an onlooker, witnessed its accomplishment
by a French gentleman whom he describes as a
superb rifle shot.   The stags, no doubt, were shot
in the ordinary manner, but the salmon, a fish of
about 10 lbs., was driven out of a pothole and shot
from a high bank, through the head, as it dashed
downstream over a swirling shallow.*

In North America, in the country south-east of
Fort Dodge, on the small tributaries of the
Cimarron River, a strangely assorted bag was made
with rifles and guns in October, 1872.   The party
consisted of Colonel R. I. Dodge of the U.S. Army,
a brother officer, and three Englishmen, and in a
hunt of twenty days they bagged the following† :

127	Buffalo (Bison)	1	Blue Bird.
2	Deer	6	Cranes.
11	Antelopes	187	Quail.
	(Prongbuck).	32	Grouse.
154	Turkeys.	84	Field-plover.
5	Geese.	33	Yellow Legs
223	Teal.		(Snipe).
45	Mallard.	12	Jack Snipe.
49	Shovel-bill.	1	Pigeon.
57	Widgeon.	9	Hawks.
38	Butter-ducks.	3	Owls.
3	Shell-ducks.	2	Badgers.
17	Herons.	7	Racoons.
143	Meadow Larks,	11	Rattlesnakes.
	Doves, Robins, etc.		

Total   1,262

* "The Field."
† R. I. Dodge : "The Hunting Grounds of the Great West" :
1877 : p. 118.

South America has little to offer the hunter of big game, and it would not be to everyone's taste to engage in the pursuit of the wild vicugna or vicunia, the llama-like animals that inhabit the high Andes immediately below the snow-line. Mr. Lydekker has given an interesting account of the hunting of these strange creatures. He writes as follows*: "The Indians hunt vicunias by forming a circular enclosure of stakes connected by cords, with a diameter of about half a mile, and an entrance of some couple of hundred feet in width. The cords connecting the stakes are hung with bright-coloured pieces of cloth, which flutter in the wind and prevent animals from trying to break through. When the enclosure is ready, the hunters made a wide circuit on the mountains, and drive in all the flocks of vicunias there may be in the neighbourhood; the animals being despatched by the bolas —a weapon consisting of two large balls connected by a string, which is whirled round the hunter's head and then hurled with unerring aim at his victim. The flesh is divided among the Indians, but the skins belong to the priests. The wool, although small in quantity, is fine and of excellent quality; and in 1826 a law was made that the vicunias should be caught and shorn, instead of killed, but the wildness of the animals rendered this impracticable. In the time of the Incas vicunia-hunts, in which as many as thirty thousand men took part, were organized upon a large scale. An area of some twenty miles would be completely surrounded, and every living thing driven in; and it is said that at times as many as forty thousand head of game, including bears, pumas, foxes, deer, vicunias, and guanacos, would be thus surrounded. Such a hunt would last for a week, during which many hundred head of game would be killed, Tschundi mentioning that in a hunt which he joined, upwards of one hundred and twenty-two vicunias were slaughtered ".

Australia is another country that has little in the way of big game, though the kangaroo affords various forms of sport. In areas where these animals had become so plentiful as to be a menace to the settlers, driving on a large scale with the aid of nets, dogs, mounted men, and hunters armed with clubs has been practised. I do not know what the record bag may be, but the following account of a drive, presumably in 1897, seems worth recording*: " At a wallaby drive on the Biragaubil estate recently some eighty ladies and gentlemen participated, when,

* " The Field " : 11th September 1897.

according to the Sydney 'Morning Herald,' some miscellaneous sport was obtained. 307 kangaroos and wallabies were killed, Mr. Thomas West, of Guntawang, heading the score with 21 ".

LIST OF BOOKS CONSULTED

This list does not represent the whole of the books that have been searched. Some of quite the best works on Big Game contain little statistical matter, and only those that have yielded information for the purpose of the present volume are included in the following.

ANDERSSON, C. J.	Lake Ngami	1856
,,	The Okavango River	1861
BAILLIE-GROHMAN, W. A.	Big Game Shooting (Badminton Library)	1894
,,	Fifteen Years' Sport and Life in the Hunting Grounds of Western America and British Columbia	1900
,,	Sport in the Alps	1896
BAKER, SIR SAMUEL W.	The Albert N'Yanza, Great Basin of the Nile	1866
,,	Big Game Shooting (Badminton Library)	1894
,,	Eight Years' Wanderings in Ceylon	1855
,,	Ismailia	1874
,,	The Nile Tributaries of Abyssinia	1868
,,	The Rifle and Hound in Ceylon	1864
,,	Wild Beasts and their Ways	1890
BALDWIN, W. C.	African Hunting and Adventure from Natal to the Zambesi	1894
BARNARD, THE REV. M. R.	Sport in Norway	1864
BELL, W. D. M.	The Wanderings of an Elephant Hunter	1923
BRADDON, SIR EDWARD	Thirty Years of Shikar	1895
BRANCH, E. DOUGLAS	The Hunting of the Buffalo	1929

LIST OF BOOKS CONSULTED

BRYDEN, H. A.	The Great and Small Game of Africa	1899
,,	Gun and Camera in Southern Africa	1893
CHAPMAN, ABEL	Big Game Shooting (The "Country Life" Library of Sport)	1905
,,	The Gun at Home and Abroad	1912–15
,,	Wild Norway	1897
COOCH BEHAR, THE MAHARAJAH OF	Thirty-seven Years of Big Game Shooting in Cooch Behar, The Duars, and Assam	1908
CUMMING, R. GORDON	Five Years of a Hunter's Life in South Africa	1850
DEMIDOFF, E. (PRINCE SAN DONATO)	Hunting Trips in the Caucasus	1900
,,	Sport in Europe	1901
DODGE, RICHARD IRVING	The Hunting Grounds of the Great West	1877
DOLLMAN, J. G.	Catalogue of the Selous Collection of Big Game in the British Museum (Natural History)	1921
ELWES, H. J.	Memories of Travel, Sport, and Natural History	1930
FINAUGHTY, WILLIAM	The Recollections of William Finaughty (Privately printed in the U.S.A.)	
FORBES, MAJOR	Eleven Years in Ceylon	1840
FORSYTH, CAPTAIN J.	The Highlands of Central India	1871
FREMANTLE, THE HON. THOMAS FRANCIS	The Book of the Rifle	1901
GÉZA, COUNT SZÉCHÉNYI	Sport in Europe	1901
GLADSTONE, HUGH S.	Record Bags and Shooting Records	1922
HARRIS, CAPTAIN CORNWALLIS	The Wild Sports of Southern Africa	1839

LIST OF BOOKS CONSULTED

HODGSON, RANDOLF, L.	Big Game Shooting (The " Country Life " Library of Sport)	1905
HORNADAY, W. T.	Camp-Fires in the Canadian Rockies	1906
LINDSAY, ROBERT, OF PITSCOTTIE	The Chronicles of Scotland	1814
LITTLEDALE, ST. GEORGE	Big Game Shooting (Badminton Library)	1894
LLOYD, L.	Field Sports of the North of Europe	1831
,,	Scandinavian Adventures	1854
LYDEKKER, RICHARD	The Game Animals of Africa	1926
,,	The Game Animals of India, Burma, Malaya and Tibet	1924
,,	The Royal Natural History	1894
LYELL, D. D.	The African Elephant and its Hunters	1924
MALCOLM, GEORGE, and MAXWELL, AYMER	Grouse and Grouse Moors	1910
MILLAIS, J. G.	British Deer and their Horns	1897
,,	The Gun at Home and Abroad	1912-15
,,	The Life of F. C. Selous	1918
,,	The Mammals of Great Britain and Ireland	1906
,,	Newfoundland and its Untrodden Ways	1907
,,	Wanderings and Memories	1919
MURRAY, T. DOUGLAS, and WHITE, A. SILVA	Sir Samuel Baker—A Memoir	1895
NEUMANN, ARTHUR H.	Elephant Hunting in East Equatorial Africa	1897
,,	The Great and Small Game of Africa	1899
OSWELL, W. COTTON	Big Game Shooting (Badminton Library)	1894
OSWELL, W. EDWARD	Willaim Cotton Oswell, Hunter and Explorer, the Story of his Life	1900

273

S

LIST OF BOOKS CONSULTED

PEASE, SIR ALFRED E.	Edmund Loder—A Memoir	1923
PERCY, LIEUT.-COL. REGINALD HEBER.	Big Game Shooting (Badminton Library)	1894
PHILLIPS-WOLLEY, CLIVE	Big Game Shooting (Badminton Library)	1894
,,	Big Game Shooting (The "Country Life" Library of Sport)	1905
PIKE, WARBURTON	The Barren Ground of Northern Canada	1892
POTTINGER, SIR HENRY	Flood, Fell and Forest	1905
QUERSIN, HENRI	Sport in Europe	1901
RADCLYFFE, MAJOR C. R. E.	Big Game Shooting in Alaska	1904
ROOSEVELT, THEODORE (PRESIDENT)	The Wilderness Hunter	1893
SANDERSON, G. P.	Thirteen Years among the Wild Beasts of India	1882
SCHEIBLER, COUNT	Sport in Europe	1901
SCHÖNBERG, BARON DONALD	Sport in Europe	1901
SELOUS, F. C.	African Nature Notes and Reminiscences	1908
,,	A Hunter's Wanderings in Africa	1881
,,	Recent Hunting Trips in British North America	1909
,,	Sport and Travel, East and West	1900
,,	Travel and Adventure in South-East Africa	1893
SETON-KARR, SIR HENRY	My Sporting Holidays	1904
STOREY, HARRY	Hunting and Shooting in Ceylon	1907
SUTHERLAND, JAMES	The Adventures of an Elephant Hunter	1912
SWAYNE, LIEUT.-COL. H. G. C.	Seventeen Trips through Somaliland and a Visit to Abyssinia	1900
TEASDALE-BUCKELL, G. T.	Experts on Guns and Shooting	1900

LIST OF BOOKS CONSULTED

VAN DER BYL, P. B.	The Gun at Home and Abroad	1912-15
VON HOHNEL, LIEUT. L.	Discovery of Lakes Rudolf and Stefanie	1894
WARD, ROWLAND	Records of Big Game (Ninth Edition)	1928
WARDROP, MAJOR-GENERAL A. E.	Days and Nights with Indian Big Game	1923
,,	Modern Pig-sticking	1914
WILLIAMSON, ANDREW	Sport and Photography in the Rocky Mountains	1880
WOLVERTON, LORD	Five Months' Sport in Somaliland	1894
WOODYATT, MAJOR-GENERAL NIGEL	My Sporting Memories	1923

INDEX.

A

Amen-Hotep III, 96
Andersson, C. J., Biographical notes, 78–80
       ,,   Injured by rhinoceros, 80
       ,,   Methods of hunting, 79
       ,,   One night's mixed bag by, 79
Antlers, Largest known of red deer, 162
Arco-Zinneberg, Count, 186
Ardennes, 190
Argali, Siberian, Head shot by Mr. St. George Littledale, 210
Auersperg, Prince, 200
Axis-deer, see Chital

B

Baigrè, Col., 116
Baillie-Grohman, W. A., Historical researches by, 163
       ,,   Wapiti heads obtained by, 243, 244
Baker, Sir Samuel W., Biographical notes, 50–60
       ,,   Day with buffaloes in Ceylon, 72
       ,,   Deer-stalking in Scotland, 55
       ,,   Discovery of the Albert N'Yanza, 55
       ,,   Estimate of his bag of African elephants, 56
       ,,   Favourite weapon for buffalo shooting, 72
       ,,   Forms of sport in Ceylon, 51
       ,,   Game killed in Africa, 56
       ,,   His book, "The Rifle and Hound in Ceylon,"51
       ,,   Hunting with hounds, 54, 144-146, 156
       ,,   Injured by elephant, 52
       ,,   Kills an immense rogue elephant, 53
       ,,   Kills two buffaloes with one shot, 72
       ,,   Kills four chital with two bullets, 148
       ,,   List of his battery, 60
       ,,   Narrow escape from buffalo, 69-72
       ,,   Opinion of Ceylon buffaloes, 67
       ,,   Rifles used by, 57-60
       ,,   Sambar hunting, 144-146
       ,,   Sport in Asia Minor, 55
       ,,   Sport in North America, 56
       ,,   Tigers shot by, 57
       ,,   Wapiti shot by, 56-57
Baldwin, William Charles, Biographical Notes, 133-136
       ,,   Bag for one night's shooting, 134
       ,,   List of game shot by, 135, 136
Barasingh, Number shot on the domains of the Maharajah of Cooch Behar, 151
Barker, Mr. Billy, 158
Barns, Mr. T. A., 45
Bate, Mr. Thomas, 244
Bears, Number shot on the domains of the Maharajah of Cooch Behar, 151

INDEX

Bears (Black), Bags made by driving, 148, 149
,, Nature of, 148
Bears (European), Distribution of, 224
,, Methods of hunting, 224
,, Record bags of, 225–227
,, Size of, 224
Bears (North American), Danger of hunting, 245, 246
,, Hunting with the knife, 246
,, Killing with a sabre, 249–250
,, Record bags of, 246–250
,, Varieties of, 245
Beddington, Lieut.-Col. C., 265
Beaufort, Roe-deer killed at, 189
Bell, Mr. W. D. M., Biographical notes, 18–24
,, Book—"The Wanderings of an Elephant Hunter", 22, 23
,, Buffaloes shot by, 62
,, Experience of the white rhinoceros, 90
,, Financial results of elephant hunting, 21
,, Greatest number of elephants shot by, in one day, 19
,, Greatest number of elephants shot by, in one month, 19
,, Leopards shot by, 104
,, Lions shot by, 104
,, Localities shot in, 18
,, Most disappointing day experienced by, 19
,, Most memorable experience, 20
,, Most unpleasant experience, 21
,, On African rhinoceroses, 90
,, On lions, 92–93
,, On lion hunting, 104, 105
,, Rhinoceroses shot by, 90
,, Rifles used by, 23
,, Rules of life when hunting, 22
,, Runs a herd of elephants to a walking pace, 22
,, Shoots buffaloes with, 22 H.V. rifle, 62
,, Skill as big game shot, 23, 62, 63, 104
,, Total bag of elephants, 19
,, Worst month's hunting experienced by, 19
,, Yearly consumption of boot leather, 21
,, Yield of ivory from his safaris, 20
Belper, Lady, 184, 185
Belper, Lord, 184, 185
Bewicke-Copley, Major, 108
Bikaner, H.H. The Maharajah of, 116
Bison, American, Bags of, 229, 232, 233
,, Distribution, 228
,, Former numbers of, 229–232
,, Methods of hunting, 229
Bison, European, Characteristics, 202
,, Distribution, 202–204
,, Historical notes on, 203, 204
,, Record bag of, 204
,, Two shot by Mr. St. George Littledale, 207, 208
Bison, Indian, see Gaur

277

INDEX

Blackbuck, Record bag of, 142
Blackmore, Mr. William, 231
Blackmount, Deer killed at, 181
Black-tailed deer, Characteristics, 262
,, Distribution, 261, 262
,, Record bag of, 262
Blood, Sir Bindon, 117
Braddon, Sir Edward, 143
Burn, Colonel, 141
Buffaloes, African, Danger of hunting, 61, 62
,, Destruction of, by rinderpest, 63
,, Record bags of, 62
,, Selous' adventure with two bulls, 64–66
,, Selous' experience with bull on the Chobe, 64
Buffaloes, Asiatic, Danger of hunting, 67
,, Maharajah of Cooch Behar's big days with, 74, 75
,, Methods of hunting, 67, 68
,, Number shot on the domains of the Maharajah of
Cooch Behar, 75
,, Record bags of, 68, 74
,, Sir Samuel Baker saved from one by charge of
small change, 72
,, Sir Samuel Baker's great day with, 72
,, Sir Samuel Baker's long shot at, 72–74
,, Two killed by one shot, 72
Buxton, Mr. E. N., 206

C

Campbell, Sir John, 116
Caribou, Methods of hunting, 255, 256
,, Migrations of, 255
,, Record bags of, 256
,, Varieties of, 255
Carpenetto, Count, 75, 139
Carton de Wiart, General, 154
Carver, Frank, 232
Caucasus, Mr. St. George Littledale's sport in, 208, 209
Chalmers, Mr. P. R., Pen-picture of R. Gordon Cumming, 41
,, Witnesses salmon shooting incident, 266, 267
Chamois, Historical notes on chase of, 193, 194
,, Record bags of, 194, 200, 201
,, Shooting in Spain, 200
Chital, Methods of hunting, 146
,, Numbers in Ceylon, 54, 146, 147
,, Sir Samuel Baker's sport with, 147, 148
,, Two killed with one bullet, 148
Clay, Colonel, 230
Clayton, Capt. Browne, 108
Clinton, Mr. Pelham, 141
Cobbold, Mr. R. P., Bag of tigers in 1897, 110
,, Mixed bag in India, 149, 150
Cody (Buffalo Bill), 232
Cooch Behar, The Maharajah of, Bag for a month's shoot, 75
,, Buffalo shooting by, 74, 75
,, Buffaloes shot on the domains of, 75
,, Gaur shooting by, 140, 141
,, Rhinoceros shoots, 137, 139

INDEX

Cooch Behar, The Maharajah of, Tiger shoots, 109
,,   Tigers shot on the domains of, 110
,,   Total game shot on the domains of, 150, 151
Cooper, Mr. Frank, 243
Crawford, Mr. Malcolm, 157, 158
Crockett, Davy, 253
Cumming, R. Gordon, Ability as a hunter, 42
,,   Battery used by, 43
,,   Best day's shooting, 39
,,   Book—"Five Years of a Hunter's Life in South Africa", 38
,,   Collection of trophies, 41
,,   Elephants killed by, 38
,,   Pen-picture of, by Mr. P. R. Chalmers, 41

D

Darnaway Forest, 189
Datia, H.H. the Maharajah of, 94
Defries, Mr. Louis, 124
Delamere, Lord, 100
Desborough, Lord, 182
Dibidale, Forest of, 179
Dodge, Richard Irving, Bag of mule deer by, 260
,,   Bag of white-tailed deer by, 261
,,   Mixed bag by, 267
,,   Pronghorn shooting incident, 263
Dunsany, Lord, 265
Dyott, Mr. G. M., 115

E

Edinburgh, Duke of, 125
Eland, Number shot by F. C. Selous, 131
Elephants, African, Antiquity of hunting, 17
,,   Danger of hunting, 17
,,   Herd run to a walking pace by Mr. W. D. M. Bell, 22, 23
,,   Methods of hunting, 17
,,   Record bags of, 18, 19, 44
,,   Sir Samuel Baker's experience of, 56
,,   Six killed with five bullets, 37
,,   Slaughter of, by the Van Zyls's, 44
,,   Tusks of, obtained by W. Finaughty, 37
,,   ,,   ,,   ,,   ,, A. H. Neumann, 32
,,   ,,   ,,   ,,   ,, W. C. Oswell, 88
,,   ,,   ,,   ,,   ,, J. Sutherland, 25
Elephants, Asiatic, Height of, in Ceylon, 47
,,   Largest shot by Sir Samuel Baker, 53
,,   Methods of shooting by native hunters in India, 46
,,   Number killed in India by G. P. Sanderson, 46
,,   Record bags of, 47–50
,,   Sir Samuel Baker caught by, 52
Elk, Distribution of, 212
,,   Emperor of Russia's shooting parties, 215
,,   Methods of hunting, 212–215
,,   Record bags of, 213
,,   Shooting with pointers, 216
,,   Size of antlers in various countries, 215, 216

INDEX

Elk, Swedish Royal shooting parties for, 213, 214
Elliot, Lady Eileen, 109
Ellis, Major, 108
Elphinstone, Lord, 75, 139, 239
Elwes, Mr. H. J., 190, 216
Emanuel, King Victor, of Italy, 221–223
Ezra, A., 74
Ezra, E., 74

F

Falco, Snr. J. P., 156
Falk, Hoftjägmästare, 225
Faunthorpe, Lieut.-Col. J. C., Biographical notes, 111–116
            ,,   Exhibitor at horse shows, 112
            ,,   General Wardrop on, 114
            ,,   Lions shot by, in India, 115
            ,,   Panther shooting by, 112, 113
            ,,   Pig-sticking, 112
            ,,   Skill with the rifle, 113, 114
            ,,   Tigers shot by, 111, 113
            ,,   War services, 114
            ,,   Wins Running Deer Competition at Bisley, 114
Faunthorpe Memorial Cup, 116
Fausett, Capt. Godfrey, 108
Ferdinand, Archduke Francis, 191
Festetics, Count Tassilo, 191
Fey, Mr. Jim, 94, 95
Finaughty, William, Biographical notes, 34–38
          ,,   Description of the plains of the Free State, 35
          ,,   Elephants shot by, 36
          ,,   Heaviest tusks obtained by, 37
          ,,   Largest number of elephants shot by, in one day, 36
          ,,   Quotation on danger of buffalo hunting, 61
          ,,   Rifles used by, 37
          ,,   Shoots six elephants with five bullets, 37
          ,,   Shoots seven lions in one day, 96
Fire-arms, Early Continental, 165, 197
Forsyth, Capt. J., Opinion of buffalo hunting, 67
Frederica, Princess of Eisenach, 168
Frederick III, Elector of Brandenburg, 161

G

Gallwey, Capt., 48, 49
Garbott, Colonel, 108
Gaur, Number shot on the domains of the Maharajah of Cooch Behar, 150
  ,, Record bag of, 140, 141
Gemsbuck, Number shot by F. C. Selous, 131
George I, Elector John, of Saxony, Biographical notes, 164–167
          ,,   Horns of stags killed by, 166
          ,,   Roe-deer killed by, 188
          ,,   Summary of game killed by, 164
          ,,   Wild boar killed by, 153

INDEX

George II, Elector John, of Saxony. Bears killed by, 225
           ,,   Biographical notes, 164–167
           ,,   Horns of stags killed by, 166
           ,,   Roe-deer killed by, 188
           ,,   Summary of game killed by, 164
           ,,   Wild boar killed by, 153
George V, H.M. King, 107, 108, 139
George, Landgrave John, of Brandenburg, 153, 168
Giraffes, Number shot by F. C. Selous, 131
Glyn, Mr. R. F., 238
Gödöllo, Wild boar shooting at, 155, 156
Grant, Mr. C. Macpherson, 189
Grochowlski, Count, 154
Guns, see Rifles.

H

Haigh, Mr. H. W. L., 264
Halleberg, Elk shooting at, 213
Hampton, General Wade, 246, 247
Harris, Capt. Cornwallis, 45, 78
Helmsley, Lord, 141
Hewitt, Sir John, 116
Hill, Mr. Clifford, 98
Hill, Mr. Harold D., 98
Höök, Major Berndt, 225
Howard, Colonel, 265
Hoyos, Count, 222
Humbert, King, of Italy, 200, 223
Hunneberg, Elk shooting at, 213
Hunter, Mr. J. A., 100 (foot-note).

I

Ibex, European, Numbers in Europe, 222
        ,,   Record bags of, 222, 223
Ibex, Spanish, 222

J

Jackson, General, 249, 250.
Jacobs, Petrus, Biographical notes, 33, 34
        ,,   Elephants killed by, 34
        ,,   Lions killed by, 98
        ,,   Mauled by lion, 98, 99
James V, King, 177
Judd, Mr. William, Lions killed by, 100
        ,,   Narrow escape from lion, 101

K

Kangaroo hunts, 269, 270
Keppel, Sir Colin, 108
Khan, Mangal, 110
Kinnaird Castle, 189
Kudu, Number shot by F. C. Selous, 131

INDEX

L

Langwell and Braemore, Excellence of red deer at, 181
Larsen, Karl, Elephants killed by, 43
,, Shoots seven lions in two minutes, 96
Layard, Mr. E. L., 47
Layard, Capt., Elephants shot by in Ceylon, 48
Leopards, Number shot by Mr. W. D. M. Bell, 104
,, Number shot on the domains of the Maharajah of Cooch Behar, 150
Lions, Danger of hunting, 92, 93, 104
,, Judd's narrow escape from, 101
,, Largest bag in a day made in South Africa, 95
,, Methods of hunting, 93, 94, 97
,, Record bags of, 94, 97, 98, 103
,, Seven shot in two minutes, 96
,, Sir Alfred Pease on " Riding them", 94
,, Wagon besieged by, 95
Littledale, St. George, Bag made by, in the Caucasus, 208
,, ,, ,, ,, ,, Neilgherry Hills, 209
,, ,, ,, ,, ,, Rocky Mountains, 209
,, Bag of Ovis Poli made by, 209
,, Biographical notes, 206–211
,, Discovers bison in the Caucasus, 206
,, Ibex shooting in the Caucasus, 223, 224
,, Shoots bison in the Caucasus, 207, 208
,, Shoots wild camels, 209
,, Skill with rifle, 210, 211
,, Trophies obtained by, 210
Loder, Sir Edmund, 182, 183, 201, 209, 210
Loder, Mr. Sydney, 182
Lonsdale, Lord, 75, 109, 139
Louis XV. of France, 169, 170
Louis XVI of France, 170
Lydekker, Richard, On vicunia hunts, 268, 269

M

Maria, Governess of the Netherlands, 168, 169
Massow, Baron, 74
Maukiewicze, Wild boar shooting at, 154
Maximilian, Emperor, Biographical notes, 195–199
,, Skill with cross bow, 196, 197
,, Sporting establishment of, 199
Menzies, Mr. W. Steuart, 266
Millais, Mr. J. G. Caribou shot by, 256–258
,, Life and work of, 258, 259
Minto, Countess of, 109
,, Earl of, 109
Mixed bags, in India, 149, 150, 265
,, in North America, 267
,, in Scotland, 265–267
Mosscoondie, Pig-sticking at, 157–160
Montgomery, Buffalo shooting incident, 63, 64

INDEX

Moose, Distribution of, 236
  ,, Head obtained by G. J. van Heek, Jr., 218
  ,, Heads obtained by A. S. Reed, 237, 238
  ,, Methods of hunting, 236, 237
  ,, Number of, in Alaska, 238
  ,, Record bag of, 237
  ,, Shooting with one arm, 239
Moritzburg, Collection of antlers at, 162
Moscicki, His Excellency M. Ignacy, 154
Mule-deer, Characteristics of, 259
  ,, R. I. Dodge's bag of, 260
Murray, of Lintrose, 81, 87
Myers, A. C., 232

N

Nepal, Rhinoceros shooting in, 139
  ,, Tiger shooting in, 107–109
Neumann, Arthur H., Best days with elephants, 31
      ,, Biographical notes, 26-33
      ,, Book by—"Elephant Hunting in East Equatorial Africa", 27
      ,, Elephant tusks obtained by, 32
      ,, Narrow escape in the Boer War, 30
      ,, Rifles used by, 32
      ,, Seriously injured by elephant, 29
      ,, Shoots his first elephant, 29
      ,, Skill as a shot, 32
Niedieck, Paul, 239

O

Orange Free State, Great drive of game in, 125, 126
Osborn, Professor H. Fairfield, on antiquity of elephant hunting, 17
Oswell, William Cotton, Biographical notes, 80–88
      ,, Discovers Lake Ngami, 81
      ,, Favourite weapon of, 82–84
      ,, Feeds six hundred natives for seven weeks, 87
      ,, Injured by rhinoceros, 85–87
      ,, Methods of hunting, 82
      ,, Narrow escapes from buffalo and lioness, 84
      ,, Narrow escape from white rhino, 84, 85
      ,, Pen-picture of, 82
      ,, Results of his elephant hunting, 88
      ,, Sport in India, 81
Ovis Poli, Littledale's bag of, 209

P

Paget, Colonel Arthur, 102
Panthers, Lieut.-Col. Faunthorpe's shooting of, 112, 113
Paris, Mr. George, 159
Patiala, H.H. The Maharajah of, 156
Pease, Sir Alfred, Lion shooting on farm of, 95
      ,, On "riding lions", 94
      ,, Rifles used by, 210
      ,, Wide experience of, 95

INDEX

Percival, Mr. A. B., Lions shot by, 101, 102
Percy, Major Algernon Heber, 206
Pig-sticking, 112, 157–160
Pike, Warburton, on caribou hunting, 256
      ,,   on caribou migration, 255
Portland, Duke of, 181, 182
Potocki, Count Constantin, 216
  ,,   Count Joseph, 155
  ,,   Count Paul, 154, 155
Pottinger, Sir Henry, 216
Pronghorn Antelope, Characteristics of, 262, 263
        ,,   Methods of hunting, 263
        ,,   Record bags of, 263

Q

Quagga, Number shot by Baldwin and his hunters, 135

R

Rabbits, 264
Radclyffe, Major C. R. E., Game killed in Alaska by, 251
      ,,   Moose shot by, 238
Radziwill, Prince Charles, 154
  ,,   Prince Jerome, 154
Rainey, Paul, 97
Ramsay, Sir Henry, 110
Rath, Charlie, 233
Red Deer, Acclimatization of, in New Zealand, 183, 184
  ,,   Bags obtained at Munkacs, 176
  ,,   ,,   ,, at Spala, 174, 175
  ,,   ,,   ,, in Spain, 176
  ,,   Historical notes on chase of, 161–170, 177, 178
  ,,   Number killed at " Blackmount," 181
  ,,   ,,   ,, " Strathraick," 181
  ,,   Record bags of, Continental, 163, 170, 171
  ,,   ,,   ,, New Zealand, 183–185
  ,,   ,,   ,, Scottish, 177, 182
Reed, Mr. A. S., 237, 238, 239
Reindeer, Distribution of, 219
  ,,   Methods of hunting, 219, 220
  ,,   Record bags of, 220
Rhinoceroses, African, Anderson injured by, 80
      ,,   Danger of hunting, 76–78
      ,,   Decrease of, in South Africa, 89
      ,,   Finaughty and Gifford's sport with, 88
      ,,   Numbers formerly in South Africa, 88
      ,,   Oswell injured by, 85–87
      ,,   Record bags of, 78, 88
      ,,   Major Stigand injured by, 45
      ,,   White species, 78, 88–90
Rhinoceroses, Great Indian, Number shot on the domains of the
                Maharajah of Cooch Behar, 150
      ,,   Range of, 137
      ,,   Record bag of, 137, 138

INDEX

Rifles (and smooth bores), First sportsmen to adopt .256 Mannlicher, 210

,,   Low-velocity, 264
,,   " Rook and Rabbit", 180, 265
,,   " Sharp", 233
,,   Used by Sir Samuel Baker, 57–60, 72
,,   ,,   ,, W. D. M. Bell, 26, 62, 104
,,   ,,   ,, Colonel Clay, 239
,,   ,,   ,, R. P. Cobbold, 110
,,   ,,   ,, W. Finaughty, 37
,,   ,,   ,, R. Gordon Cumming, 43
,,   ,,   ,, King Humbert of Italy, 200, 201
,,   ,,   ,, Karl Larsen, 43
,,   ,,   ,, St. George Littledale, 210, 211
,,   ,,   ,, A. H. Neumann, 32
,,   ,,   ,, W. C. Oswell, 82–84
,,   ,,   ,, Sir Alfred Pease, 210
,,   ,,   ,, Major Rogers, 48
,,   ,,   ,, Duke of Saxe-Coburg-Gotha, 172
,,   ,,   ,, F. C. Selous, 128
,,   ,,   ,, Colonel J. Stevenson-Hamilton, 104
,,   ,,   ,, J. Sutherland, 26
Roan Antelope, Number shot by F. C. Selous, 131
Roe-deer, Four killed at one shot, 192
,,   Heads at Vienna Exhibition, 187, 191
,,   Historical notes on chase of, 186, 187
,,   Number killed on Continent, 186
,,   On islands of Danube, 191
,,   Record bags of, 188–191
,,   Shooting from canoe, 191, 192
,,   Swedish, 192
Rogers, Major, Elephants killed by, 47, 48
,,   Guns used by, 48
Roosevelt, Theodore (President), on bear hunting, 245, 248–250
,,   on pioneer hunters, 252–4
Ross, Edward, 179
,, Horatio, 178–180
Royal Hunt of Sweden, 213, 214
Rudolf, Crown Prince, of Austria, 191
Russell, Sir Baker, 108
Russia, Emperor of, 174, 189, 190, 204, 215

S

Sable Antelope, Number shot by F. C. Selous, 131
,,   Three shot with one bullet, 135
Sambar, Sir Samuel Baker's hunting of, 144–146
,,   Methods of hunting, 144
,,   Number shot on the domains of the Maharajah of Cooch Behar, 151
,,   Record bags of, 144
Saxe-Altembourg, Prince Albert of, 205

INDEX

Saxe-Coburg-Gotha, Duke Ernest II of, Bag for one year, 173, 174
,,   Biographical notes, 171–174
,,   Chamois shot by, 201
,,   Horns of stags shot by, 171
,,   Red deer shot by, 171
,,   Skill as a shot, 172, 173
Schepetowka, Roe-deer shooting at, 190
,,   Wild boar shooting at, 155
Schwarzenberg, House of, Game killed on estates of, 176
Selous, F. C., Adventure with two buffaloes, 64–66
,,   Biographical notes, 126–133
,,   Collection of trophies, 130
,,   Elephant-gun used by, 128
,,   Horse injured by buffalo, 66
,,   Lists of game shot by, 131–133
,,   Natural History Museum Memorial, 130
,,   On danger of rhinoceros hunting, 76, 77
,,   Reindeer hunting, 221
,,   Summary of expeditions, 129
Sen, P., 74
Seton-Karr, Sir Henry, On Pronghorn shooting, 263
,,   Wapiti heads obtained by, 243
,,   Wapiti hunting experiences, 244
Sikh ex-soldier, Lion shooting by, 99, 100
Simpson, Sir Benjamin, 139
Skinner, Capt., Elephants shot by, 48
Smith-Dorrien, Sir Horace, 108
Spala, Imperial forest of, 174
Stevenson-Hamilton, Col. J., 102, 103
Stigand, Major C. H., 45
Sutherland, Mr. James, Biographical notes, 24–26
                       Book—"The Adventures of an Elephant
                         Hunter", 25
                       Elephants shot by, 24
                       Heaviest tusks obtained by, 25
                       Narrow escapes of, 25
                       Rifles used by, 25
,,   Mr. J. G., 184
Svensson, Jan., 226
Swayne, Colonel H. G. C., Career of, 119–124
,,   Explorations by, 123
,,   Mauled by lioness, 120
,,   On predatory cats, 121
,,   On statistics of sport, 122
,,   Tiger shooting incident, 117–119
,,   War services, 124
Tarifa, Duke of, 156

T

Tarnowski, Count Z., 191
Teano, Prince, 75, 139
Teck, Duke of, 108
Teleki, Count Samuel, Buffaloes shot by, 66
,,   Rhinoceroses shot by, 91

INDEX

Thott, Count Stig, 192
Tichborne, Sir Henry, 75, 139
Tigers, Distribution of, 107
  ,,   Habits of, 106
  ,,   Methods of hunting, 106, 107
  ,,   Number shot on the domains of the Maharajah of Cooch
           Behar, 110
  ,,   Record bags of, 107–111
  ,,   Col. Swayne's incident with, 117–119
Trauttmansdorf, Prince Charles, 187
Tsessebe, Number shot by F. C. Selous, 131
Turin, Count of, 75, 139
Tyskiewiez, Count B., 154

U

Umfolsi Reserve, 89

V

Van der Byl, P. B., On black bear shooting, 148, 149
            ,,   Reindeer stalking, 221
van Heek, G. J., Jr., 217, 218
Vardon, Major Frank, 81, 91
Vernay, Mr. Arthur S., 115
Vernay-Faunthorpe Expedition, 115
Vicunia hunts, 268, 269
Viljoen, Jan., His party's bag of elephants for one season, 44
      ,,   Reputation as an elephant hunter, 43

W

Wallaby drive, 269, 270
Wapiti, Distribution of, 240
    ,,   Record bags of, 241, 242
    ,,   Slaughter of, 241
Wales, H.R.H. Prince of (H.M. King Edward VII), 213
Walker, General W. H., 230, 231
Ward, Lt.-Col. A. E., 111
Wardrop, Maj.-Gen. A. E., 106
Watson, Mr. Hall, 75, 139
Wells, Sam, 263
West, Mr. Thomas, 270
White-tailed deer, Methods of hunting, 260
         ,,   Record bag of, 261
Whittal, Mr. H. O., 209
Wilczek, Count, 222
Wild Boar, Characteristics of, 152
      ,,   Hunting of, with hounds, 156
      ,,   Methods of hunting, 152–155
      ,,   Pig-sticking records, 157
      ,,   Record bags of, 153, 154
      ,,   Shooting in Spain, 156
      ,,   Size of, in Volhynia, 155

INDEX

William IV, Duke, of Bavaria, 188
Williams, Mr. John, 181
Williamson, Mr. Andrew, 241-243
Winans, Mr. Walter, 178
Wolkowycki, Colonel, 154
Wolverton, Lord, 102
Woot de Janée, Baron de, 190
Wright, Mr. W. H., 250
Würtemberg, Dukes of, 168

Zillerthal Alps, 200

www.ingramcontent.com/pod-product-compliance
Lightning Source LLC
Chambersburg PA
CBHW020352100426
42812CB00001B/33